The Oxford and Cambridge
may anthologies 2000

SHORT STORIES

Varsity/Cherwell

Varsity Publications Limited, 11-12 Trumpington Street, Cambridge CB2 1QA

Published by Varsity Publications Limited 2000

This collection © Varsity Publications Limited 2000

ISBN 0 902240 29 3

A CIP catalogue record for this book is available from the British Library

Typeset by Rachel Flowerday
Printed and bound in Great Britain by Origen Production Limited

Original concept: Peter Davies, Adrian Woolfson, Ron Dimant

All rights reserved. No part of this publication may be reproduced, stored in a retrieval system, or transmitted, in any form or by any means — electronic, mechanical, photocopying, recording or otherwise — without the prior permission of the Publisher. Copyright on individual stories reverts to author on publication.

Further copies of this book and others in the series can be obtained through all good bookshops or direct from Varsity Publications Limited, 11-12 Trumpington Street, Cambridge CB2 1QA.
Telephone: (44) 01223 353422
Fax: (44) 01223 352913
Email address: business@varsity.cam.ac.uk

Website: www.varsity.cam.ac.uk/Anthologies

may anthologies 2000

Editors: Sophie Levy (Cambridge)
                     Tom Rob Smith (Cambridge)
                     Catherine Shoard (Oxford)
                     Peter Robins (Oxford)

Executive Editor: Lawrence Norfolk

Publisher: Rachel Flowerday

Cover Design: Shehani Fernando, Rachel Flowerday

Cover Photos: Shehani Fernando

Editorial Committees

Prose: Matt Applewhite
         Jo Goulbourne
         Trisha Gupta
         Maartje Scheltens
         Debs Stansfield
         Zoë Svendsen

Poetry: Sarah Cain
         Ruth Fowler
         Wendy Lee
         Douglas McCabe
         Betty Messazos

Selection co-ordinator: Ajesh Patalay

Launched 5th May 2000 at Waterstone's, Cambridge

Other titles available in this series:

The May Anthology Short Stories 1998
selected and introduced by Sebastian Faulks

The May Anthology Poetry 1998
selected and introduced by J.H. Prynne

The May Anthology Short Stories 1999
selected and introduced by Penelope Lively

The May Anthology Poetry 1999
selected and introduced by John Kinsella

The May Anthology Poetry 2000
selected and introduced by Paul Muldoon

also available from Varsity Publications Limited:

From Our Cambridge Correspondent
Cambridge student life 1945-95 as seen in the pages of ***Varsity***, the Cambridge student newspaper. By Mark Wetherall

Cambridge Through Student Eyes
The essential guide to the historic city of Cambridge, written and produced entirely by students. Third Edition

Thanks

College sponsors

Cambridge:
Churchill, Clare, Darwin, Emmanuel, Fitzwilliam, Gonville & Caius, King's, Lucy Cavendish, Jesus, Newnham, Pembroke, Queens', Robinson, St. Catharine's, St. John's, Selwyn, Sidney Sussex, Trinity

Oxford:
Christ Church's Christopher Tower Fund, Hertford, Jesus, Linacre, Magdalen, Oriel, St. Peter's, The Queen's College

Thanks also to Carole Blake, Dr Michael Franklin, Paul Muldoon, Sophie Craig, Ben Yeoh, Jon Travers, Jill Hocking, Isobel Dixon, Phillip Wells, Adam and Liz at Waterstone's, Melony at Corpus Christi, Diana Tapp, Joti and Debbie, Graduate Advisers at Natwest, Ken Barnett & Origen Production Ltd and Suzanne Arnold for their assistance, and everyone who submitted work

contents

Contents

Introduction	Lawrence Norfolk	1
Sloebake	Simon Stirrup	3
Stub	Richard Williams	35
Whiskers on Kittens	Rachel Tripp	55
Rocketman	Meg Vandermerwe	71
Voices Are Different	Frank Shovlin	85
Livelihood	Alex Lawrence	91
Tango	Tamar Landau	103
Blood Lilies	Stephanie Frank	119
Last Light	Catherine Totty	143
Contributors		161

Introduction

Here are nine stories. Two mad scientists duel in the desert, a future-world gunslinger passes the job-interview from hell, a schoolgirl dumps the friend in a million, the moon pulls a boy into inner space, a sniper finds he cannot join the party, the oldest woman in the world engineers a long-anticipated death, a widower learns to dance, two fading Southern belles wilt with the flowers they supply for other people's weddings, and in the ninth I have yet to decipher either what happens or what it means but I was convinced by it, as I was by all the contributions collected here, which is enough.

And difficult enough too. Fiction tends to prolongation and a good short story is an exercise in stringency, and perhaps self-denial. No-one wants to wield the scalpel on their own creation, but that is what the form demands. Technique matters.

The tonal range of these stories spans comic-book macho, clear-eyed world-weariness, arch irony, and sheer unapologetic enigma. They stood out from the submission because their authors knew what effect they wanted and did not hedge. Conviction again, and a sense of self-belief amongst their writers. After the prose and punctuation, the metaphors and mouthiness, after the well-turned phrase and the twist in the tale — all *that* — fiction is a game of nerves. No-one here flinched.

Lawrence Norfolk

Sloebake

I wake on the morning of the third day and sit up stiffly. The iron beneath me is already starting to heat up, and it feels like I'm sitting on a giant hotplate, spattered and crusted and dumped out here in the dirt. I look around. The laboratory complex is a shantytown, a rusting island on a calm sea of dust, and for the moment I can't remember how I got here. The desert is everything. It stretches as far as I can push the sphere of my perception, and I absently wonder if there is anything else.

But I was waiting for something.

I stand up painfully, joints clicking as they slowly thaw from the cold night, and shielding my eyes like a TV castaway I scan the arid bowl around me. The wind hangs dirty veils of dust across a horizon that shifts slowly as if painted there by a delirious mind, and the heat haze is already starting to build. As I watch the dust clouds are caught up and carried high, and there are set aflame by the newly risen sun. The brilliant circle burns purple when I blink, and I realise that I've been staring too long.

I turn a slow three hundred and sixty degrees, mesmerised by the pattern of rutted and baked earth that surrounds me. The desert is a dead allotment, and I'm standing here on a cracked and overturned flowerpot, right in the middle.

A localised wind picks up and takes some of the heat away. My head is thumping with dehydration and moving is painful, but move I do and with an effort I come to the edge and piss concentrated urine in a dark golden arc off the roof, watching it make a damp impression in the earth below. It stings, and I sit down heavily. I wish I was a desert rat pissing crystals, knowing that not a drop was wasted.

Three days up here; it's starting to tell. In the morning the sky looks deep and cool and ready to dive into, but as the heat builds it fades into haze and lights dance around the edge of vision.

I brush some dead skin from my shoulder and watch it fall like unlooked-for desert snow into the deep canyons of the corrugated roof. I feel like a part of it now, pitted and flaking and just about ready for the scrapyard.

I rise again and stand with hands on hips. I'm waiting…

They should be here soon. Here to collect us; Sloebake and myself. I wonder if he's down there, prowling around like an animal, looking for me. But no, of course not.

Geoffrey Sloebake. May his fat soul rest in peace. Before this summer he was just a name to me, just a postscript in a letter, ink on paper.

He was already here when I arrived, sweating and hairy in his chair, boots cast aside and feet resting on the piano stool. I knew nothing of him, save that he was the only other scientist out here for this season, and that he had been assigned to help me after my failure to arrange help for myself. Shaking his hand was like grappling with an array of soft and yielding marine sponges, and I remember wondering if the man had any bones at all. He looked solid enough, but solid in a viscous kind of way, as if he would flow slowly rather than walk.

I introduced myself, acutely aware of the antique aeroplane that had brought me here rattling noisily back into the sky outside. As I spoke my name he eyed me appraisingly, then closed his spongy fingers tight round mine and pulled me down to the level of his soft face.

"Sloebake," he mouthed. I mumbled something more and he released me. As I was dragging my trunk up the stairs to my room he shouted out:

"Best get an early night my boy; plenty of work for tomorrow." I waited for a few seconds, expecting some kind of explanation, but he just sat sagging in the chair, looking out through the window at the red desert, and I realised that I had been dismissed.

The research station had been built for something like two dozen researchers, but it was old now, and flaking, and most people went to the new centre, two hundred miles to the north. I suppose what ended up here was the dregs of the scientific community, crippled children left outside the mountain when the door closed. But that's overly dramatic — there simply wasn't enough room at St Martin's, and anyone not allocated a place had to come here or go home. This year it was Sloebake and myself, both crippled in the head in our own ways, and nobody else. I suppose you could say that fate brought us together.

The complex had been built with facilities to deal with most kinds of desert fauna, but our interest was nothing more demanding than the termites that built their towers locally. I was intending to collect them and to study their behaviour, to see how they worked together to construct such monuments, and as I understand it Sloebake had submitted an application that ran almost word for word with mine. We were to spend three months at the station, and the rusty thrumming of engines that came like a bookend on either side of this period was to be our only contact with the world.

Peace, I had thought. Three months of solace and earth and red desert quiet and nobody to disturb me, as if by leaving it all behind my mind would be washed clean. But you can't just go off researching all over the place with nobody to look out for you, and you looking out for no-one — it is not permitted for a person to be left alone in the station. Sloebake had valuable experience.

You will notice that I say had.

He hasn't got anything now, not a scrap of adipose tissue left on the fucker. I was about to say "bless him," but that would be unseemly; I can only assume that he's got relatives somewhere, although the more I ponder that the more I come to wonder if he was not just spontaneously created out of some kind of effluvial ooze.

But my thinking is getting confused, I'm jumping ahead. Termites, it was, that I was talking about. Surprisingly little work done in such an interesting field, not even any reliable estimates of colony size. This and much more I told myself in the long idle months of my convalescence, leafing through journals and trying to forget. I accepted my arguments without too much protest — anything to get out and away. I came to regret that arbitrary decision, but no matter. Termites are colonial foragers, building huge freestanding structures of earth and excavating radiating networks of tunnels around them. These networks can be anything up to 200 metres in diameter and —

Sets the scene, doesn't it? Three months of that, three months of mark-release-recapture and tiresome lab colonies and sweat. Don't get me wrong, I'm as scientifically minded as the next scabby lab-rat, but my experience was somewhat soured you see.

That first night I was nervous, unnerved by the uncommunicative fat man downstairs and apprehensive at being so far from home when the furthest I had ever previously been was Italy, and that a degrading field-trip. I unpacked my trunk slowly, feeling almost shell-shocked by the sudden changes and nursing a dry cough that had been building all day. The room was spacious — it had probably been top-dogs only before; a luxury kennel with ceiling fan and sunset view, but it was old now, and the fan creaked alarmingly above my head as I laid out my clothes on the clean linen.

I considered exploring my new home. I had seen the extent of the complex from the aeroplane, a child's table-top composite of upturned yoghurt pots and cereal boxes realised in decayed concrete on the desert's red carpet, but from the ground, set against its flat surroundings, it had looked monumental. I had a free run of the place — all the facilities were mine to command, but I was tired and I could hear Sloebake stirring downstairs. I had only just met him, but already he seemed almost like an animal to me, and I feared meeting him in a narrow corridor, pressing forwards like a sandstone block to seal me in.

I decided on an early night, but before turning in resolved to be out-going in the morning. Perhaps I had seemed unapproachable to him — if he was a seasoned researcher he might not have had much human contact in the last few years. I promised myself to make an effort to make friends and then turned out the light.

I rose early and took a shower in the *en suite* bathroom. The water was heated in a solar installation outside, and after the freezing desert night it ran in tepid, oily-feeling beads over my body. I dressed in a cool cotton shirt and slacks and descended the creaking stairs into the combined kitchen and common room where I had met Sloebake the previous evening. There was no sign of the man, so I found powdered milk and settled down to a breakfast of scratchy cornflakes and weak orange cordial.

The bulk of the food at the station was kept in long, low storage huts outside that ran over the north-east quarter of the compound like corrugated-iron worms laid out in the sun by some curious child. They were mostly disused now, and the supplies supplied to Sloebake and myself had been stashed in one end of the nearest hut to our rooms. We had enough stores of canned and vacuum-packed foods to last us double our allotted time, even with Sloebake's remorseless appetite. As I chewed my cornflakes I suddenly caught sight of him out of the window.

He was walking back and forth in the dust, each dragging footstep stirring up a little red cloud of it, and as he walked he whirled a spade around in his hands like a nightmare cheerleader. I watched him as he moved, his great head sunk in formless shoulders, the spade spinning around his fat fingers in a disc of dull wood and reflected metal. His feet barely lifted from the ground, and from a distance he almost seemed to be gliding up and down in the dirt, a monstrous hovercraft patrolling a dead beach.

On the about-turn of his circuit he sighted me through the glass and glided over, spinning his spade and whistling tunelessly. He wrenched the window open, admitting an intense gust of hot air and scattering small fragments of fused rust and paint onto the floor. He eyed me as I desperately tried to swallow the cereal so that I could say something, then grinned and opened his mouth in a wide yawn.

"Let me show you around," he said.

I left the cornflakes to set in their bowl and stepped out into the heat of the early morning. Sloebake was already crossing the expanse of cracked and weed-grown concrete that had served as a parking lot when the station was inhabited, and although he was barely ten metres away the shimmering air made his image dance and flicker like a genie that should have stayed in its lamp. I tried to ignore the sagging architecture of his body as he ploughed on ahead of me, but the sparse trappings of the desert seemed to focus my attention on him. With his form blurred and distanced by the heat haze it was as if some great baroque cathedral had uprooted itself and set off to wander the desert, shedding more gargoyles and arches as it climbed each dune and leaving a trail of pitted masonry in its path, anticipating the day its last fleshy buttress was devoured by the scouring sand.

Sloebake was heading for an old jeep that for some reason he had parked on the far corner of the crumbling lot, and when I caught him up at the door of the vehicle he pointed down at the concrete with pride. In yellow paint that was already fading he had designated a parking space with dashed lines, and stretching along one side of it, blazoned in big, sloppy capitals, was his name. I removed my boot from the terminal 'e' of Sloebake and climbed up into the passenger seat, wondering if the man was retarded, or psychotic. This rusting army-surplus junk, with Sloebake the self-appointed captain, seemed to represent the entire compound — isolated and becalmed on a dead sea of dust.

The jeep was old and windowless, but the smell of stale beer and Sloebake's stale sweat had still permeated everything and I was relieved when Sloebake started the engine and we rolled off into the desert. We were following the remains of a dirt track that the scientists had cut in previous years, and I could see the line of compacted earth snaking off across the dips and rises ahead of us.

"Where are we going?" I half-shouted across the noise of the engine and the wind that pushed at my face through the gaping front window. Sloebake pointed out across the hills to a level area about five miles distant.

"I'll show you the field where the mounds are," he said, "and we can collect some samples."

He patted the handle of the spade that was now riding

between us, the shining blade resting against the base of the gearbox.

"You've been out there before?" I asked, my voice shaking as the jeep plunged into a small ravine cut by some long-dead floodwater.

"A few times now. I've been at the station for over a week; I think you'll by quite impressed by what we have here."

I looked again at the area Sloebake had indicated earlier. The plain was shrouded in mirage and wind-blown sand, but straining my eyes it seemed that there were dozens of needle-like towers scattered across the ground. From that distance it was as if the earth had melted and dripped upwards into a heavy sky, only to freeze again, capturing the massive stalagmites as they reached for heaven.

I glanced over at Sloebake, lost in a reverie of grit and heat, propelling the disintegrating vehicle across the desert by sheer willpower. His manner had changed dramatically, at the same time lifting my spirits, and I decided that his mood the day before had been just a short-term reaction to my appearance in his kingdom. He whistled softly as we crossed the red sea of dunes that lay between the research station and the field of towers, and I sat back and tried to remember all that I could about termites.

Fifteen minutes later the jeep bounded over the last dune and started down the gentle slope that led to the plain. The sand graded smoothly into a muddy red and crumbling earth, and directly ahead, shockingly close now, was the first of the towers.

It was perhaps twenty feet high, a ruddy composite of desert earth and stones and sticky insect spittle. The surface was smooth, but the construct as a whole seemed to have been chiselled by some giant hand, its lines and contours forming an astute parody of a human church or skyscraper. The sun was high now, but the base of the monolith was caught still in a deep pool of shadow that extended thin fingers up the tower's flanks like an emaciated lover. I had read of these things, even seen photographs in an old issue of National Geographic, but the scale staggered me and for a moment I could not speak.

"Phallic, isn't it?" leered Sloebake as we passed through the shadow of the tower. I nodded my agreement and absently wondered if that was what had drawn the man here. I ran my forefinger along my upper lip thoughtfully.

"How many are there?"

"Here?" he waved his left arm expansively, "About seventy-five on the plain — little more, little less. It is hard to tell."

He made a show of peering out of the front window. The menhirs were flourishing in this dusty garden, sprouting where nothing else but a few creosote bushes could. I noticed that no two towers were within a hundred metres of each other, and I imagined the radiating foraging tunnels that spread like fungal mycelia from each rusty hub, seeing the dark tendrils pushing outwards under the earth.

We saw many dead colonies as we progressed across the field. Deserted towers eroded quickly in the savage winds, and their jutting forms dotted the plain like broken and rotted teeth. At times it felt like we were in the mouth of a giant, his hot breath blowing in through the jeep windows and carrying our sweat away.

We drove towards the northeast corner of the plain, which I could see clearly now was ringed by dunes, and soon I became aware of a colony directly ahead that was almost twice as high as any of the others. It reached up with bloodied hands, the petrified priest of some long-dead sun cult. From what I had read of the towers I judged that it was probably well over a hundred years old.

The structure was broad at the base, and rose upwards in a series of tiers and buttresses that came together in a peak high above the floor of the basin. From our position in the jeep it looked inert and dry in the way that a mountain does — aloof high above the teeming world, but I knew that under the surface it teemed itself. The mountain was burrowed through with tunnels and thoroughfares all thronged with arthropod life.

Sloebake cut the engine a few metres from where the monolith rose sheer-sided out of the desert floor and pulled on the ageing handbrake with a low grunt. He stepped down from the cab with surprising grace and stalked off across the bare earth, hefting his spade across his shoulder. Eagerly, I climbed down and half-ran after him.

"This is the chief mound round here," he called back to me once he stood under the tower on its sunlit side. The bright light fell obliquely on his face and gave it a sweaty sheen, picking out every feature. As I approached him he lifted the spade and hewed at the tower, sending rusty fragments pattering to the dust. He continued till he found them, white and swollen and surrounded by their teeming siblings.

"Grubs," he declared, "get the sample pots."

As I ran back with the plastic containers he was scooping the larvae out onto the earth with cupped hands.

"Some say you can eat them," he said, then spat thickly into the wounded flank and kicked the dust up with his heels. The grubs lay in a writhing pile on the ground, and I hurriedly gathered them up as Sloebake hacked his way deeper into the mountain, exposing a tracery of tiny tunnels punctuated by the larger nursery chambers. Pieces of hardened mud rained onto my shoulders as Sloebake hit out with increasing ferocity, as if determined to fell this deformed and leafless tree. I stood quickly and grabbed his arm as he prepared to swing again.

"What are you doing? We have enough." I motioned to the mature termites that walked dazedly around my feet, and held the full sample pot under his nose.

"The Queen!" he shouted, then flung the spade in exasperation and stalked back to the jeep. The spade embedded itself in the moist earth of the interior, then fell after a few seconds and pulled more debris after itself as it slid to the ground. Concerned that Sloebake would drive off and leave me there I collected some mature samples and headed back to the jeep.

He sat sulking in the driver's seat, his fat hanging off him like dripping wax, as if his flesh was bulging through some half-formed exoskeleton. He looked like the king of all grubs, cradled in worn leather with a crown of matted and filthy hair. He didn't say a word as I climbed back into my seat and put the spade down between us like a token of truce; he just gunned the engine and sent us speeding back across the red hills.

I feel like I am swimming through soup up here. My journal is in the compound somewhere and all this, that happened barely two months ago, seems like something remembered from a film seen in childhood. I can only accept with some difficulty that it was I standing under that carmine monument, and the images I see are flickering and crossed by dark lines.

Some things I can remember clearly though. Some things float in the soup like under-cooked and unwelcome butterbeans, full of sourness and bile.

More and more these days I find myself looking to the roof for comfort and support, as if it were an old friend, but I find it is iron and pitted, and it jabs me with rust as I fold again and lie curled in the heat. If they don't arrive soon it will be too late for me as well, and all they shall find up here is a piece of charcoal with expensive binoculars around its neck. I feel welded here, bones stuck down with tissue that has liquefied and spread and dried out in the sun. I feel like the thinnest of oily films, with dust collecting on my surface, and when the rains come I'll be carried to an underground cave where my bones will rest on a bed of sand. I realise, holding one scorched claw in front of my eyes, that I must look a state.

But I suppose that this is the culmination of a long ambition for me. When I was recovering before, during the long months of my stay in hospital, I'd felt myself withdrawing further from the abrasive world of humanity, my mind bulldozing its bustling urban districts so that my mental country was once again free from language and relationships. Like an animal, or a baby. Confined to my hospital bed I wandered through my own skull, and as the cities receded or fell into ruin I felt my claustrophobia lift. Every tasteless meal and every tasteless conversation drove me further away, another civilisation falling in my mind, and not even the feel and smell of the young nurses as they changed my dressings could bring me back.

Looking back, I think that what I was seeking in coming here was a compensation for all the privacy that I had lost over the years — the ultimate solitude of a dusty red womb, and the kind of peace that I had not known since my difficult birth.

Very early on I realised that he had been sent to thwart me, an emissary from my own past sent to sabotage the present. When all that I wanted was to explore the wasteland that was an extension of my own mind, Sloebake stalked me and staked out the limits of my compound in rusting beer cans and spittle-flecked earth.

Many times I came back sweating from fieldwork and found an empty fridge, and him gorged and motionless on the sofa with legs dangling like a butcher's display. I often felt like kicking him, slapping his fat face and shaking him to waking, but always I turned and walked hungry and dry up to my room. He would wake during the night, and finding himself sprawled on the floor would roar and go crashing about the room, scattering chairs and table in a bleary rage.

There was no lock on my door, although the fresh paint could not hide the marks where one had been, and a week after I had been at the compound Sloebake burst in during the night and sat on my bed, quizzing me about my past in a drunken voice. The next night I barricaded the door with my trunk, and a few nights after that he tried it again. The heavy wooden box was wedged firmly between the door and the end of bed, and when he found he could not enter he pounded the door with his fat fists and screamed.

"Honking freak! Twigful pole! Just a filament you are, just frayed string. I will scorch you!"

I sat terrified in my bed, fighting the urge to jump out of the window and run, but after five minutes he left and took the shotgun from downstairs. I heard the jeep start up and then he was gone till the morning, scattering lead shot over the desert. The dull, distant explosions coloured my sleep that night, and I woke feverish, just before dawn, thinking that I heard voices in the long empty corridors.

On other nights he came and just sat outside the door, sometimes for hours on end, and I heard his strained breathing as I tried to sleep. I grew to fear him more and more as the weeks went by, seeing his violence and temper, and his venom for that dusty place.

I stand again, and it hurts like merry hell. My skin feels like it's hanging off in strips and that's probably not far from the truth; my arms are shiny red and crusted with dead skin and blisters like limpets. It's getting harder and harder to move at all, and I'm thankful that I didn't bring a mirror up here. I think of the shady places inside the compound, right below me, but just the anticipation of climbing down drains my energy and I nearly stumble. There are pains beside my sunburn — my twisted ankle, my shrunken stomach — but these are dim and I am barely aware of them most of the time.

Everything is deadly quiet up here. When Sloebake was around there was always noise; even when asleep he was noisy. But now the jeep lies silent and half-wrecked where I left it on a dune to the west, and Sloebake's heavy presence has been lifted. The only sound besides my stertorous breathing is the scraping metallic whine of the windmill as it spins and drives the underground turbines, and even this ceases when the breezes fail. I can see the flicker of the blades out of the tail of my eye, whirring round on top of their blotchy pylon.

But now there is a difference. The noise of the windmill seems to go down in pitch for a second, then returns to normal, as if some deeper component is struggling to reach me through a strong wind. I listen carefully, wondering if my delirium has returned, but soon the sound is back; distant, very distant, but now discernibly coming from a separate source. I gaze across the heat-fuddled land, noticing for the first time the dark patches where my retina has been burnt out, and after a couple of minutes I see what I have been waiting for.

So they are coming at last.

And why not before? I could have called for help weeks ago and been airlifted from this rusty cradle, but when I first came here I searched high and low for the radio and found nothing. There should be one, of that I am certain, but when I questioned Sloebake about the matter he put a clumsy fat finger to his nose and laughed, then denied all knowledge of. Idly looking through his possessions after his death I found one of the corroded old dials in a draw, although the rest of it has never shown up. Why he dismantled it I don't know, but somewhere at the back of my mind I know that I would never have left anyway.

But now our tenancy is up and I am to be escorted out of here. I might have some explaining to do.

My relationship with Sloebake was always ambiguous. Sometimes he treated me like a kid brother, showing me this or that with a strange glow of pride, but mostly he persecuted me; bullying and ridiculing and making me carry out meaningless tasks.

As for our research — I got on with mine and he with his. I was beginning to make some theories about communication working with small groups in the lab, but with Sloebake around it was slow and laborious work. To this day I have no idea what he was working on; he took wheeled curtains from the old medical ward and walled off a personal laboratory for himself, and one night shortly before he died he destroyed all his notes. He was supposedly conducting similar research to myself, but although I saw plenty of termites disappear into his ephemeral workshop, as far as I know none were ever repatriated. I remember once naïvely suggesting that we work together on a population estimate project, only to be laughed down and treated like a cripplehead for the rest of the day.

Two weeks after my arrival I was working in the lab,

encouraging termites from neighbouring colonies to work together using a generic pheromone solution I had concocted. Sloebake's deep voice burst suddenly from my short-range walkie-talkie, wrapped in static. He sounded out of breath and genuinely agitated.

"Found a sag-rat boy," his voice moved in and out of focus as I crossed the room to where the device lay on a scarred bench-top. Sag-rat was the local name for an indigenous species of desert marsupial somewhere between a cat and a pony. They were rare; for some reason their rumpled skins were prized hunting trophies, and population sizes had been falling for the past fifty years. I found a latent excitement rising in my belly. Just as I reached the bench the radio erupted into life again.

"It's alive," more static, then "injured though, quite badly. I ran over its legs."

This made me groan, but I wasn't at all surprised. Before I could remember how to send my voice back to him he was with me again, his voice broken into rough shards by the frenzied electrics.

"There's \\\\\\\\\\\\\\\\\\\\\\\\\\-andstorm, //////////////////-oming back now. Get read-\\\\\\\\\\\\\\\\\\\\\\" and the handset fell silent.

With the benefit of hindsight I have no doubt that even this breakdown in communications was somehow contrived by Sloebake. During my long delirium I deified the man, attempting to suck the raw power from his bones with my rituals, but even now I am convinced of his potency.

Accepting the radio as a dead loss I hurried into the derelict medical ward and cast about, trying to find anything that could save the creature. I spent a full hour setting up a bed with a drip and searching for useful supplies that would not unbalance the animal's metabolism. I explored the ward thoroughly, tripping over abandoned crutches and ancient rolls of swabbing, and when I was done I sat exhausted in the station's padded dentist's chair. I fell asleep waiting, lulled by the darkness and the intermittent whirring of the windmill. When Sloebake returned, some hours later, he was without sag-rat, and scorned any suggestion that there had ever been one.

I was apoplectic, and ran into the lab intent on tearing down his makeshift partitions and exposing his work. Half way across the floor a heavy glass sample jar hit the back of my head and shattered, and I awoke around midnight, the left side of my face stuck down with caked blood. I avoided Sloebake for days after that, creeping around the station and panicking in the long empty corridors.

I tried to avoid Sloebake as much as I could in general, but he seemed almost to hunt me, and always knew exactly where I was. His heavy tread and heavier hand on my shoulder were enough to set up pin-pricks of sweat on my forehead, and I often flushed in anticipation of some new humiliation in his presence.

One morning a blocked drain forced me down to the communal showers, and I walked there fully clothed through the early chill. The station was becoming more and more dilapidated — in previous years a modest maintenance staff had been kept on, but with just the two of us here it was not deemed a priority. The desert scorched the halls and outhouses during the day and froze them at night, cracking paint and peeling it off in long strips. The plumbing was disintegrating around us, and the kitchen taps often discharged a rusty brown solution in lieu of water. The network of dying pipes sounded off at night, clanking and shrieking as it contracted after the heat of the day, and at times the station vibrated with a sound like the death-call of a beached whale.

I picked a cubicle two-thirds of the way down the long hangar and ducked inside, making sure to lock the door after me. I undressed in the cramped darkness — I had no idea how to route power to this part of the compound — and stepped into the shower's lukewarm embrace.

I was soaping my scalp when I heard him burst through the double swing-doors at the far end of the hall. He worked his way down the long line of deserted stalls, and I heard the crack of each door as it slammed back and into the partition. It was a charade entirely for my benefit — the splashing water must have instantly told him where I was, and I decided to spoil his game.

"I'm here Sloebake," I called above the water, "did you want something?"

Marching feet, and then a sudden crash as the door of my cubicle burst free of its lock and was thrown open. I held the clammy curtain to my chest like a disturbed adulterer and blinked in the half-light. Sloebake stood, literally blocking the doorway, and eyed me with contempt.

"The jeep's acting up," he said, as I rubbed the soap from my eyes. "We'll have to hike to the towers."

"Well, I don't actually need to go down today anyway," I said, and tried a gracious smile. "Why don't —"

"Hiking!" he roared, and dented the plywood partition with his huge fist. I nodded feebly and he sloped off, turning at the end of the hall and adding, "forty minutes!"

So we hiked. Forty minutes later I was standing in the ruined car park with a small khaki pack at my feet and sunglasses pushed up above my hairline. Sloebake's improvised parking space was empty, and I assumed that he was attempting to repair the jeep in one of the forsaken workshops at the southeast corner of the compound. It was only ten in the morning, but already my brow and upper lip were collecting sweat, and I lowered my glasses to shut out the brightness. The world was shrouded and looked suddenly subterranean, and through the gloom came Sloebake, a mammoth from some crude cave drawing come to life and prowling his dark prison. Even through the polarised filters I could see the sun reflecting off him, and the muted light sprang from his sweat-slicked skin like an array of fragile crystals, advancing and retreating in radial patterns as he moved.

I have never known anyone who sweated as much as Sloebake. Even in our quarters where the ceiling fans were still functional the slightest effort brought a sickly sheen to his face and arms, and I often fantasised about trapping him in a sauna and watching him melt away. His pores must have been bacterial wishing wells, and his stale smell permeated everything.

I came out of my reverie to find him bearing down on me like a tank, scattering loose gravel chippings from under his feet as he scuffed his heels along the ground, and staring straight at me. He was wearing a ragged T-shirt and a huge, shapeless pair of shorts, and he carried just a single water flask slung around his neck.

"Ho, scrote!" he hailed me, "we've got a walk ahead of us." He wiped sweat from his brow and flicked it onto the concrete, then made a sharp turn and headed for the perimeter of our coarse garden. I felt my shoulders sag, but I knew that I could not afford to turn my back on him. I picked up my bag and walked into the dusty cloud kicked up by his shuffling feet.

It took us two-and-a-half hours to walk the five miles to the field of towers. Sloebake had to stop and rest at the top of every dune, and as we walked he was constantly blotting his face with a faded paisley handkerchief. We stuck to the dirt track as far as it went, stumbling over the sun-hardened wheel ruts and saying little. As we struck off from the path after about half an hour I raised my eyes from the desert's rocky floor and looked out towards the basin. I had been there perhaps a dozen times since my arrival, but the hazy vista of great earthen menhirs still filled me with a sort of primitive awe, like a cro magnon blinking in the corona half-light of an eclipse. From this distance the towers seemed to be formed up in ranks, like the starkly uniform markers in a war cemetery, each one a silent testimony to innocence lost.

Within the next two miles Sloebake had collapsed at the crest of a high dune and emptied the last of his water over face and neck, very little actually ending up in his mouth. Realising the can was empty he threw it away behind him, where it tumbled end over end down the dune's flank, sending up little red clouds as its strap whipped the arid sand. Sloebake watched it morosely over his shoulder, then turned to me with mock-pleading in his eyes. Sitting there with his legs stuck out straight and the spilt water pooling around his buttocks he looked like a morbidly obese and slightly backwards child causing trouble at a friend's birthday party.

"Water," he said, and held out a hand like a baseball glove.

"Not much, Sloebake," I said, handing him my canteen, "this has got to last us there and back again. Maybe we should call this off and —"

While I was talking he took a long drink, then emptied the rest of the water out into the thirsty sand. It disappeared immediately, leaving nothing but a damp crater behind it. I rushed forward to stop him, but he held me off and sent the bottle spinning; it landed twenty feet off and followed its predecessor down the dune. The last drops of water were spread out in a glittering arc that fell to earth and rolled down the slope in a hundred dirty balls before the desert took it. I was dumbstruck, and gaped at Sloebake like a cretin.

"Don't need water," he said, "plenty of water here," and he patted his swollen belly. I raised my fist to strike him, but he put one massive hand on my chest and propelled me backwards down the mercifully shallow far slope. My head was jarred as I hit the ground and the sand rucked up around my thighs. I wanted to run away, but the compound was my only home now, and with a dim fear I remembered Sloebake's shotgun. I picked myself up and, turning my back to the laughing figure on the skyline, set off for the distant basin.

I was parched by the time we mounted the last dune, and Sloebake, despite all his boasts, was suffering badly. His T-shirt was stained with darkly spreading rings around the armpits and broad vertical flashes on his chest and back, like the insignia of a filthy army. He gripped the back of my neck with his moist fingers and leaned on me so that I stumbled and nearly pitched headfirst down the sandy hill. His breathing sounded like a metalworks in my ear, and I walked off in disgust.

I had already decided to collect my unwanted samples from the nearest colony and then to rest a while in the shade before setting off again. Sloebake, however, was adamant that we head for a larger monolith five hundred yards ahead, in spite of his obvious discomfort.

"They're different there," he said, panting, "red ones, blue ones..." and he moved off at a renewed pace. I felt like collapsing, but fear and doggedness and a morbid curiosity drove me on, somehow animating my tired sinew and bone.

When we reached the tower I found that it was unusually wide around the base, and began noting down dimensions estimates in my ring-bound sketchbook. Sloebake fell into a pile on the ground and didn't move as I took a small trowel from my pack and started an excavation of the colony's periphery, exposing each tunnel like a surgeon working on a tricky vein. I was aware of him watching me, his small eyes burning through the soft dough of his face, and then he laughed and stood up, like a grubby tenement block demolished in reverse.

"Nature calls," he said, grabbing at his groin, then bounded off around an outflung wing of the tower that seemed to hang in the air like a spectral curtain. I was immediately suspicious, and stood stock-still as he disappeared behind the tower's dark outline. Minutes passed, and I stayed exactly where I was, a dwarf before a ruddy mountain laced with black veins of shadow. I knew that he was plotting something, and I half-expected him to appear climbing over a shoulder of the mound, or maybe even to burst through its brittle outer crust and attack me with flailing maggot arms. Another minute passed, and I was just deciding to ignore his prank when I heard the whine of a starter motor and a second later, the dull roar of an engine.

The jeep careered around the great buttress of earth and the rusting mudguard caught me in the ribs and threw me backwards into the dirt. I heard Sloebake's laugh over the rattle of the engine, and then both were gone.

I lay on the scorched ground and cursed him. Two of my ribs were broken, and it was over an hour before I could stand up fully and start the long hike back to the compound.

I'm lying on my front now, trying to conserve any strength I have left for when they arrive, for when I have to make myself known. I'm resting scabbed elbows on the scabbed iron and holding the binoculars with both hands; they feel like a part of me now, an attachment slotted into my ocular orbits and rusted in place, feeding me a jaundiced view of the world.

The plane's coming down fast and I can make out the

pilot behind his strengthened glass. It tears along the dusty airstrip like it's actually going through the earth, kicking up a hanging cloud to shield its newborn trench.

I'm nearly dead. I can feel the life squeezing out of my pores and burning off in a purple mist. They'll reach me soon, but until then I'll stay here, punctured by hot little needles and holding my life in. Through the binoculars the plane looks suddenly funereal, with a plume of black feathers like spurting crude springing from the cockpit and wavering in the breeze as three gaunt figures step down onto the thirsty ground.

It was perhaps a month after I first arrived at the research station that Sloebake drove me out to the termites' plain for the last time. At ten he was drinking tequila and by eleven he was drunk, steering an erratic course across the desert that looped and backtracked like the coils of a fallen length of rope. As the jeep sailed from the top of each dune I dug my nails into the passenger door's rubber handle and cursed Sloebake, but he was enjoying himself and smacked my hand away when I tried to grab the wheel.

He had brought his shotgun as well as his spade this time, and it rested between us like a statement of unspoken hostility. Sloebake laughed much but said little, and every now and then he reached out and touched the weapon's heavy barrels as if checking that it was still there. I was relieved when we finally pulled up in front of the largest monolith, the one that I had seen on my first trip there.

Sloebake almost fell from the cab, then steadied himself against the tarnished doorframe and retrieved his gun and spade. I hopped down on the other side and shouldered my pack, wanting to start work and forget about the fat man that tormented me.

We started digging, and as we worked Sloebake kept

up a constant monologue, shouting into the dry air.

"I like to work with a hard-on," he said, slinging a spadeful of earth over his shoulder extravagantly, "makes me feel powerful, makes me feel like a man!"

He carried this on for another few minutes as I tried to ignore him, and eventually he tired of his own voice and remembered his tequila. He drove his spade into the dry earth with a solid sound and left it standing, its blade barring tunnels and disrupting dozens of chemical trails.

"Drink, boy," he said, his voice as blurred as his vision must have been. "Bring my bottle!"

"Get it yourself," I said wearily, and went to carry on loading my plastic tray, but Sloebake snatched up his shotgun and started roaring.

"Bring my bottle, orphan, or I'll tan your hide for you; leave you flapping and swinging my flag! Tie you at half-mast and shoot you down!" He levelled the gun at me and I ducked out of the way. His laughter followed me back to the jeep, and I spat on his seat as I fumbled in the glove compartment.

I found his bottle and took it back to him. He downed a third of the sickly-looking liquid at once and then wiped his mouth in an exaggerated manner and sighed.

"See what you miss, cakehater? See what you have lost? I could shake you down all right. How do you move boy? How do you —"

I pulled the spade from the ground and hit out wildly. The blade caught him full across the side of the face and he fell instantly, sprawling on his belly in the dirt. I hit him twice more on the back of the head and his blood spread a dark patch on the ground.

I stood for a few seconds breathing hard, then fell to my knees by his side and moved my hands in slow circles around his head, as if feeling an invisible barrier. After a few seconds more I picked up the bottle that was bleeding out into the dirt and staggered back to the jeep.

I drove back fast, my released anger blazing a trail across the wasteland with the little jeep a meteor at its head, and when I reached the carpark I spun the vehicle in a tight arc that scattered gravel ahead of it like an advancing wave-front. I had been drinking on the way, and the empty bottle lay discarded on the passenger seat as I scoured the station's stores and warehouses for more. There was a crate of whiskey in one of the peripheral outhouses, along with tall stacks of beer cans that Sloebake had obviously discovered long ago. I sat on a wooden crate and opened a new bottle, a derelict king holding court with his phantoms, and within another hour I had blacked out.

I woke collapsed against a wall of wooden boards that were beginning to splinter and buckle outwards under my weight. My throne was broken open and I lay in a wreckage of smashed glass and balsa, with whiskey pooled around my legs and vomit dried into my shirt. My forearms were cut and slashed, and as I stood up a dull white bomb went off behind my eyes and I reeled into a stack of canned food.

It was dark in the outhouse, but the sunlight that found its way between the desiccated planks was strong, and stamped the dusty floor with solid bars of amber. It was past noon, and I slowly realised that I had been prostrate for many hours, and a cold desert night had passed since I had attacked Sloebake. I hurried to the kitchen and swallowed five aspirins, then knocked weakly on the stained wood of Sloebake's bedroom door. There was no response, and after a minute or so I gingerly tried the handle. It was locked, but looking through the keyhole I had an unobstructed view of Sloebake's empty bed, the creased and grimy sheets hanging down onto the floor like a discarded shroud.

I was shaking, and had to sit down for five minutes before I could continue with my search. Sloebake wasn't in the lab or the kitchen or anywhere else that I looked, and at half-past-one I abandoned the crumbling hulks of the compound and set off for the field of towers.

I was on the edge of panic, and the empty tequila bottle on the passenger seat pointed at me like an accusing finger. I sent it flying out over the sand, but still I felt Sloebake's oppressive presence in the jeep, as if the sweat soaked into the ancient leather upholstery was sentient, and was surrounding me with its malicious will.

It didn't take long to find him in the end. He had crawled on a small distance after I left, moving himself into the shade of the tower, and his wide, dragging trail was clear on the ground; a pictogram painted in sunlight and blood and disturbed earth. Sloebake himself was lying on his back next to a gash in the mound, and from a distance it looked like the desert had melted and bubbled up and then set into a great dusty dome that sprang from the earth like an ulcer.

I was reluctant to approach him as I stepped down from the jeep, but curiosity more than anything else spurred me on. A cloud of flies flew up as I reached him, and one look told me that he was dead. His head and shoulders were gummed with blood, and his eyes stared straight upwards as if looking for deliverance that had never come. The wall of the tower next to him had been gouged with fat fingers, and his open mouth was crammed with the grubs that he had tried to survive on. I don't know exactly how he died — it may have been exposure or the head wounds, or just a simple loss of blood. The ground around him was stained dark, as if he lay on a cloth of his own design that I could wrap around him for his journey to the morgue, but Sloebake was not going anywhere. It would have half-killed me just to manhandle him into the jeep, but I realised that he could not just be left out in the open.

Using the last strength I could find I took up the spade that still rested where Sloebake had fallen and hacked at the rusty wall by his head. It took over an hour to cut an alcove big enough to shove him into, but I knew that there was no need to pack the earth back in around him; the termites would soon rebuild their fortress.

When I was done I turned my back on the man that I had hated so much and turned my face to the warmth of the sun. I was exhausted and weak, and when I reached the station again I collapsed onto the mess room sofa and slept soundly.

I passed the next three weeks in a thick and febrile soup, and I can remember little. Sorting through my papers I have found sheets dated within that period, but they are just reams of numbers and gibberish, and what it was that I was trying to prove I cannot say. When I try to look back all I see are dim images of the lab and the desert, but they are confused and fragments of the machine I built find their way into the red towers so that they bristle with retort stands and broken glass rods.

I climbed some of the colonies, I think. I can see myself moving up hand over hand, each footstep caving in a nursery or a larder. I flattened a little platform for myself at the apex of each mountain, and sat there for hours in silent commune with the desert, my ragged shirt tied around my waist.

The machine is still in there, somewhere beneath me in the lab, but I haven't ventured in there for days and I have forgotten nearly everything. All these images are murky and uncertain, and in my mind the desert looks like a bad film set, so that I find it hard to believe my own accounts.

Whatever happened in that time, my next clear memory is of standing again in front of the mound; Sloebake's earthy mausoleum. I exhumed him with my spade — the termites had been busy and the wound was healed, patched over with red dirt and all knitted together with the little fuckers' spit. I opened the earth wall up with great swings of the spade, its blade cutting with a crunch, scything great gashes and scattering dirt in a red cloud. Once the hole was there I dropped to my knees and started digging with my hands, pulling great chunks of the outer crust away until I found him.

The termites had been busy indeed, and there was not a scrap of meat left on him. He looked diminished there, sticking out of the red dirt in so many pieces, and I realised that his power was gone. I pulled out all the bones I could find, loaded up the jeep and scattered them in the desert, breaking him up as much as I could so that he could never come back. I kept his pelvis till last, and sent it spinning like a dinner plate off the highest dune I could find. I watched it till it rolled out of sight, then turned the jeep and drove off into the red evening, leaving a trail of disturbed earth and dusty bones behind.

That was three days ago, and I've spent the rest of my time up here waiting for them. I can't go back into the complex now; there is too much badness there, and the supplies I hastily gathered in my terror have nearly run out, but they are coming, the three of them moving like angels across the stony ground. Salvation is at hand, and I gather my strength as it approaches.

As the first figure reaches the near edge of the old carpark I hang from the guttering on the edge of the roof and drop onto the ground, the binoculars dragging my head down and forcing me to my knees with their inertia. The left lens shatters on a stone and I throw the expensive toy away. The aeroplane's crew have heard the noise and there's apprehension in their movements now — they probably noticed that there was no luggage or cargo stacked outside when they landed, and they've grouped together, each one scanning the flaking outlines of the compound with narrow eyes.

I look terrible I know — shaggy and hairy and burned with the skin hanging off me in flakes, but I limp out of the shadows towards them, shouting weakly and waving my arms. They've seen me and they come running. One slows as he sees the state I'm in and now stands warily, saying something and gesticulating with blurred hands. He has had a haircut recently, and the short hairs on his neck bristle out erect to form a soft creeping aura over his sweating skin.

The others arrive and the leader says something more; his lips move and words emerge only to hang there in billows before the wind carries them away. I smack the nearest one feebly across the ear and he looks annoyed. There's more talk, then he takes my wrists gently and the other two go inside. He's quite a young man and his grip is strong. He sits me down on the earth and suddenly my head is too heavy to support and I'm lying on my back paralysed and it feels like I'm dying. I can feel water being trickled into my mouth and he's talking still, bending over me and murmuring, but it's not him that I'm looking at but the sun as I lose consciousness and the world is suddenly washed out with white light.

"/////// — out here on your own —"

*

*

"////////// — somebody fucked up real bad —"

* * *

Cool cotton sheets and strip lighting.

It wasn't me that killed him, it was my subconscious. If I'd woken sooner I would have saved him, but I slept past midday and he was dead on arrival. I can't be held responsible for that any more than I can be held responsible for what I dream at night.

I can't feel guilty about that.

They found no trace of him, and I have heard nothing about any official enquiry. I told them on the plane that he had wandered off into the midday heat and that was the last that I had seen of him, but the young man just wiped the sweat from my face and told me to calm down. It all seems very long ago.

I open my eyes and suddenly I'm in a world of pale pastel walls and quiet air-conditioning; a quiet ward with silent sisters wheeling gleaming trolleys like robots. But I've seen all this before, and it feels like I've been here for months. Mr Charleston in the bed next to mine is snoring again and I hope that he'll die soon; the only time that I get any peace is when he's out on one of his lawn-walks.

I think about looking at one of my National Geographics again, but I'm too tired and I just stay where I am, staring up at the flawless ceiling. The sister smiled when I asked for the magazines and said something about dedication, but I find it difficult to concentrate on what anyone is saying these days. I'll have another research post soon, and then I can discharge myself and be on my way again. The desert burns in me, and the city outside my small window seems lacklustre and sickly, all dull deadened surfaces and empty faces. I've applied for posts all over the globe; it's just a matter of time now.

I can feel myself withdrawing further from the scorching world of humanity, and not even the feel and smell of the young nurses as they change my dressings can bring me back. Every tasteless meal and every tasteless conversation drives me further away and sees another civilisation fall in my mind. It won't be long now.

Simon Stirrup

Stub

I could see them both from where I sat, the two dark figures crouching in the shadows. They had stalked one another for an hour now, round and round the mining settlement, sneaking quietly between buildings, senses alert, waiting for a stray sound or smell to betray the position of the other. Now, it seemed, the end was at hand. One of them was huddled down on the ground, peering between two battered yellow cargo containers. He was scanning the open ground barely visible through the crack, hoping to catch a glimpse of his quarry, but there was nothing. I saw him shift his weight and edge sideways a fraction, so he could scope the rest of the buildings. As he did a stud on his belt grazed the hard metal surface of the crate, and his enemy, a few paces behind him, took the opportunity to ease himself a little farther around the corner.

The huddled one looked down at the stud. A wire-thin strip of yellow paint twirled away from its point. The silver line of fresh metal glinted back in the darkness. Then he realised, I don't know how, he realised the danger he was in. I saw his body clench as he strained his ears for the softest brush of skin on cloth, of someone else's breathing suppressed to almost nothing. His eyes slid sideways in their sockets and he gripped his gun tighter.

There it was, the swipe of skin on skin, of an arm being brought up to fire. All pretence aside, he dropped forwards, boots kicking up dust, and rolled to his back. He whipped his arm around until he was staring down the barrel straight into his enemy's eyes. Their gazes flashed across one another for an instant before they both inhaled savagely, gasping for every last bit of air,

"BANG! BANG! BANG! BANG! BANG! BANG! BANG!"

The pieces of piping jerked in their hands as the vocal bullets spat forth. Once again, their chests heaved as they cried in perfect unison,

"GOT YOU FIRST!"

Another game of 'Outlaws and Watchmen' ends, the same way they always do. The kid standing had dived at the one on his back and they were wrestling on the ground. Their "guns," pieces of scrap, had been forgotten, as the two settled their argument in a far more physical manner. When I looked back at them, one nearly had the other pinned, who, in turn, grabbed the tuft of hair on the other kid's head and slammed it down. Young skull met hard dirt with a thud and the struggle continued,

"You're DEAD!

You MISSED!

Did NOT!

GET OFF!"

I didn't know their names, but I knew who they were. I'd been the same a few years ago; creeping through settlements, hunting my friends. We thought we were just like the gangers that came through town everyday, either trading at the post or lounging in the bar, and every single one with a gun strapped to their hip or slung over their back. The mark of a warrior, that set them above all the rest of us.

They all knew, whether consciously or not, that no one makes it in the Underhive without one thing.

Respect.

To get respect, you have to fight.

To fight, you need a gun.

Even we Goliaths know that. The biggest, the strongest of us would never go into a fight without packing something. It was kind of comforting to me when I was a kid, my little rebellious thought whenever some seven foot, man-mountain of a ganger ordered me to fetch this or carry that. You may be larger than me, you may be louder, but without that piece of metal stuck in your belt, that piece of metal that looks so ridiculous when your oversized fingers are crammed around it, you would be nothing.

I remember the feel of having a gun in my hand, even a make-believe one. To only have to point, to kill, as if I were the Emperor himself. Now it was going to happen, today was the beginning. I ran a hand over my shaven head, already I could feel stubble, the tops of stiff hairs poking through the skin. I wanted to look my best, nose stud polished up, my hair freshly dyed. Trying to look like the warrior that I would become, if the gang judged me worthy. There was only one thing missing, on my belt hung a knife and a holster, an empty holster.

I tried to relax, tried to calm down, waiting for them to get started with whatever. After all I couldn't look too wired, they might think I'm scared. I dropped my head back on the pile of iron slag I lay against, staring up at the faraway ceiling. Then again, it would be worse if I looked like I was snoozing, or day-dreaming. I shifted onto my side and propped myself up on my elbow. I squirmed to try and find a comfortable position among those sharp little rocks. A flash of pain stabbed through my side. I looked down. My braces had got twisted, the studs that lined them were digging into my flesh. Clambering to my knees I began adjusting the few clothes I was wearing, making sure everything sharp pointed outwards and looked keen, rather than pointing inwards and being... inconvenient. Distracted, I didn't notice the shadow fall across me. I sure noticed the meaty hand dropped on my shoulder, though.

I didn't shoot up, that would have been the worst thing to do. I knew who it was. The harsh metallic grating of respirated breathing and the edge of Second Best mingled with stale sweat in the air left me no doubt. It was the ganger sent to test me. First impressions matter, he'd caught me off guard and if he saw me jump out of my skin he'd know I wasn't up to it, might even refuse to let me try. I didn't know whether he could do that or not, but I wasn't taking any chances. So, instead, I let him wait a second, like I knew he was there all along, and then I turned my head, slowly.

His hand gave him away. He was old. It's always the hands that show it best. He must have been nearly forty. Long past his best, still just a ganger, with no hope of ever becoming anything more. He had become everything a young man dreaded. No wonder he reeked of cheap Second Best. I got up of my knees and his antediluvian limb fell away. I swung around to him. His head was shaven and the respirator covered most of his face. No, his head wasn't bare by choice, he didn't have any hair at all. I tried to stop staring at his gleaming dome. He didn't flinch his gaze. His scarred and hairy body still looked powerful, the two pistols hung at his belt and the studs and spikes and the ammo chains on his clothes would have made him an impressive figure indeed. As it was, though, I couldn't help but feel embarrassed to see such a man.

His hands rose to his face and his thick fingers undid the straps on his respirator with practised ease. He pulled it to the side of his face, revealing a gold ring through his nose and an old, faded tattoo on his cheek. His lips twisted and words emerged in his low, damaged voice,

"You ready?"

We hadn't walked far from the mining town before he stopped in front of me.

"This is it."

What was it? The place was deserted, nothing apart from a pile of planks dumped nearby. What was the test supposed to be, single combat? Fine by me, I guess, I would just have to be careful not to kill the old man. He glanced back at me and must have seen fear instead of confusion.

"You better not be wasting my time, juve. You still wanna do this?"

"Yes, sir," I snapped back instinctively and hated myself for giving him the respect he didn't deserve.

"Cos it's easy by me if you wanna quit. Save me waiting around for you."

I held my mouth in check. I didn't trust what would come out. He finally turned away and padded over to the planks. He crouched down and fumbled for his respirator. After a drag he took a hold on the top piece and heaved. Nothing moved. I couldn't believe it, even a piece of recyc-plastic was too much for this guy. No one could be that puny, yet there he was, he wasn't grunting or anything but I could see the strain through his body, his muscles rippling along his back and the trembling of his head. Suddenly an almighty crack resounded around the plain and the old man shot up. He stood back and I peered at what he had left behind. The plastic plank had snapped in two, and this wasn't cheap package plastic either, but the reinforced kind. It had been bolted to the stone in the floor. I was stunned. Looking back on it, he could have weakened it before he collected me, or maybe it had already been damaged. But that didn't stop me reconsidering my opinion of him. He took another breath through his respirator, then let it hang to the side as wiped away a bead of sweat that had formed on his brow. If he noticed the change in my expression, he didn't show it.

"This," he announced, pointing at the planks, "is what you're gonna do."

Suddenly, for the first time, I wasn't sure whether I would make it, whether I could match such a feat.

"This leads straight into one of the mine shafts."

Now the broken plank had shifted I could see that it had covered a small hole beneath. It looked like it dropped straight down but, in this light, I couldn't see more than a few feet.

"This shaft used to be worked, along with the others. But it got infested and the rock-worms inside started to come out for dinner. The locals buried the main entrance, and when they found that some of the nasties had burrowed out through this hole, they boarded it up and hoped nature would take its course, that is that everything inside would eat each other. If you want in, you go down there, you scrag one of the worms and you drag yourself back here with proof, something it couldn't live without. Get it?"

"Yes, sir."

My mind raced, digesting the information. A mine infested with milliasaurs, kill one and bring back a trophy. Simple and straight-forward, just like us Goliaths, but was I only going to have my knife? In answer to my unspoken question the ganger pulled one of the pistols, a stub gun, from his belt and offered it to me. My breath caught with anticipation.

"Here. Take this."

I did so, with a careful reverence.

"But remember, we do not need such things. We are Goliath. Where others are weak, we are strong. Where others rely, we merely use."

His grotesque voice carried on with its dogma. I'd heard it often enough. I concentrated instead on the magnificent object I held in my hand, a G40K revolver-style stub gun, standard product of the Goliath heavy industries. Cheap, hard to break, easy to repair, there were thousand weapons identical to this one in Hive Primus alone, and countless millions of variants on the design across the planet. But as my fingers curled around the moulded plastic grip and brushed against the trigger I knew this one was unique, because there was only one of that multitude that was in my hand. I hefted it and felt its comforting weight. I slid it into my holster and it fit perfectly. I let my hand rest on my hip, tensed in anticipation. The quickdraw. My arm leapt forward, the pistol in its grasp nothing more than a streak of silver. I aimed it, clenched one eye and looked straight down its barrel. I felt the power, the power of life and death of whoever crossed those sights. A red shape blocked my vision. Suddenly I was hauled from the ground. I dangled from my bracers which were sandwiched between the gnarled fists of the ganger. His eyes displayed his lack of amusement.

"Get it?" he demanded.

"Yes. Yes, sir," I stammered in response, my feet struggling in the air.

He snorted and released his grip. I felt the drop jar all the way up my body and collapsed to my knees in front of him, coughing in the dirt.

"You will."

I fell the last few feet or, at least, I would have done if my belt hadn't caught on a small metal spur poking out of the tunnel wall. The moment I spent hanging in mid-air, suspended by my trousers, screwed up my timing and so, when the inevitable happened, I clattered to the ground, landing one limb at a time.

I'd shot to my feet, whipped the pistol from its holster and was scanning my surroundings for danger before my brain kicked in. I have to admit, after the wave of adrenaline had broken over me and my pulse settled down, that I felt pretty smug about that recovery. Yeah, I'd looked a fool but that happens sometimes and all the smooth moves after, pure instinct. After years of playing, it felt so natural to be doing the real thing.

A spark flashed across my eyes, jolting me from my self-congratulation and illuminated the dimly lit area. The sharp odour of ozone briefly overwhelmed the underlying smell of dank stone and rusting metal. It was a storage room, if the crates and barrels were anything to go by. The main support column in the centre of the room had collapsed, more than that, it had been virtually felled by the explosion that had collapsed the tunnel entrance. As a result most of the other end had caved in. The sparks flared again. Something had been ripped off the wall; circuitry had been exposed.

There was only one way out, apart from the hole above my head, of course, and, as I put my gloved hand on the frame to look through, I discovered what this means of egress had been, a window. It crunched and I felt, not pain exactly, just the threat of imminent pain if I gripped any tighter. Ever so gently I peeled my hand away and brushed away the pieces of glass embedded in my glove. Keeping well clear of the jagged edges, I leaned forward and peered down. It was quite a drop but, lucky for me, there were stacks of containers that would make the descent easier. I eased myself through the gap and moved onto the topmost box. It moved with me. With ponderous inevitability the stack gently began to topple away from the wall. Quickly I jammed my other foot back to steady the pile and rocked it back. Regaining my balance, I grudgingly tucked the pistol back into its holster and used both hands to lower myself cautiously down. Damn, I assumed the crates would be full, it never occurred to me that the miners would have emptied everything before they left, just as they had stripped whatever had been of use from the last room. Feet now firmly on the floor, pistol and knife in hand, my eyes searched. Nothing. Nothing but the piles of boxes and a big hole in the ground in front of me. A ladder was attached to the lip, leading down into the darkness. I slowly edged round the circumference of the opening, stub gun trained on the shadows. Nothing again, apart from this time there was the faint whiff of an effluent stream.

Once I'd got down there I had to follow the smell to find the source. Buried in the shadows in the corner there was a tiny crawlspace, as I leaned down I was hit by the reek of the sewage. It was dark, damp and a perfect place for milliasaurs. Now, you couldn't survive in the Underhive if you were claustrophobic, but everyone has limits; and having to squeeze through a passage only big enough for a child, full of the stench of liquid garbage, to hunt monstrous worms who'd paralyse you and then drag you home for a slow digestion, is getting close to mine. Still I had no choice, and I had my gun. That was enough.

I dropped to my hands and knees, then to my belly. I coughed with the extra weight on my lungs. There would barely be enough room for me to lift my head to see where I was going. I pushed my knife-sheath and holster around my belt until they were beside my hips,

I couldn't have them dig into my waist as I pushed myself along. Steeling myself, I entered, nudging my pistol and knife in front of me. With my shoulders pressed against the sides, I put arm in front of arm, then swung a hip forwards and dragged my legs along behind me. I struggled onwards. My chest scraped along the bottom, my hair was flattened against the top, it brushed dust down into my eyes, making me blink. When I finally had the full length of my body inside, I realised exactly how narrow the shaft was. My only way out would be to push myself backwards, completely blind. If something got behind me there was no room to turn around. Nothing I could do. What use would even a meltagun be if something bit me in the leg? And if it was a milliasaur, one bite would be all it needed for its poison to cripple me. My breathing quickened, I couldn't fill my lungs, I was gasping for air. My body heat reflected off the surfaces that covered me; it was hot, and the smell, I might as well have been drinking it in. I knew I was panicking, but that knowledge gave me no comfort, trapped in that monster's lair. My head was beginning to feel light. Deep breath, the thought sprung suddenly into my mind, that's what I need, a good deep breath. I stopped gasping for a second, closed my eyes and gripped the butt of my gun. Whoosh, the dust-laden, stink-ridden air was blown into my lungs until my chest had expanded so much that my back was driven into the roof of the tunnel. Then I let it flow out, until I felt quite deflated. I felt at peace for only a moment, then my nose began to itch, my head sprung back and a sneeze exploded from my face. My forehead bounced off the floor and ricocheted into the top of the shaft. My hair softened the impact but my temple throbbed. After taking a moment to recover I wiped my nose on my hand and dragged myself on.

The pool of filth gurgled and lapped against its metal banks in a hideous mockery of water. Pressed to the ground as I was, my nose was unfortunately close to it. There was no way across so I spun round on my belly and made my way back. The tunnel had opened out into the crawlspace proper, in fact, one corner of the room above had fallen in so I clambered out of it. Another storage room. A column had collapsed across it, or it could have been a beam which had fallen from the roof, whatever, it had smashed the stairs forcing me to climb along its length until I could drop off onto the floor above. I was confronted with a lift, twisted at such an angle that gave no doubt to its state of repair. I carried on, this time through a hole in the wall which led onto the rock face.

Pleased as I was that I hadn't encountered anything down in that crawlspace, I couldn't kick the feeling of... having been cheated. There should have been something there, even if not a milliasaur, rats or spiders or even a face-eater. I shuddered at the thought of bumbling across such a monster unexpectedly. Still, it was odd I hadn't seen signs of any activity at all. Perhaps, after the mine was collapsed, the milliasaurs had retreated deeper, maybe the locals had been right and the creatures had turned on each other once their ready supply of food had been cut off. Maybe there'd never been anything and the gang had put me down here because they'd already rejected me, as a joke, to go and scrag something that didn't exist. No, they wouldn't have spared the effort to tell me to get lost. I'd show them. I'd show them I was worthy of their gang, hell, I could lead their gang, given a chance.

Even as ventured on in my hunt, my mind was miles above as I sketched out my glorious career.

It wouldn't take much. After I'd passed this stupid initiation and shoved a half dozen rock-worm trophies down the old man's throat, we'd be hired to guard a Guilder trade caravan. The gang leader would have set the route, I'd have warned him that it took us too close to a fortified tower in Scavvy territory but none of them would've listened to me because I was so new. I would be ready when the first shots of ambush rang out and have sprung forwards, rushing the Scavvy raiders.

I jumped up on top of a crate to simulate climbing the tower.

They'd be surprised by how quickly I reacted and I would slaughter their leader's mutant bodyguards and put a gun to his head, demanding the rest of his ramshackle band gave themselves up. As soon as they had I would kick him off the top level,

I booted the air for emphasis,

and the rest of my gang would slaughter the rest of the degenerates. Our only casualty would be our foolish leader, cut down in the first few seconds. The Guilders would shower me with goods and cash and I would become the new gang boss.

Getting down from the crate, I continued on.

Would I be content then? With a female in one hand and a bottle of Wild Snake in the other? Hardly. I would purchase from the Van Saar techs two of their finest bolt pistols, for an exorbitant fee. They'd try to double-cross me, of course. Insist I come alone and then try and leave with both their weapons and my corpse. I would be too quick for them.

Two imaginary pistols leapt into my outstretched hands.

The Van Saars in the room would fall in seconds, before any of them had a time to draw. The rest of the gang would burst in and meet the same fate.

I crouched behind a barrel, picking off phantom

enemies with my stub gun.

Another victory, and then on and up, until I rested on a throne in the Hive City itself.

Spectral smoke coiled up from the barrel. I drew it up to my lips and gently blew it away.

High above me, a shape detached itself from the darkness and dropped. It clubbed me over the back of the head. My jaw smashed into the muzzle. My teeth howled in pain and blood spurted into my mouth. I was knocked down, hard. The stub gun tumbled away. I was stunned for a critical second, not knowing what had happened, I thought the roof was caving in. Then I looked over my shoulder into the gaping maw of the milliasaur, and I moved. Its first poisonous bite went wild as I spun onto my back. It shot back as fast as a snake, rearing to strike again. Its tiny legs stood out like horns running down the side of its rocky carapace. I saw the next strike coming and flattened myself against the ground as its incredibly powerful muscles rocketed it through the air. It didn't even bother to draw back before it struck again. It lunged forwards clumsily but there was no more ground I could give. The fangs bore down and I threw my other arm up for what little protection it could provide. The monster, seeing something shoot into its mouth crunched down early. The knife I'd held was by its teeth and it bucked away. I struggled up and scrambled into the corner, scooped up the pistol and whirled around. I planted my back foot, one arm steadying the other, looking straight down the sights. A stance perfect for the first time I would feel the power, the first time I would unleash the cold fury of this most deadly, most beautiful of weapons.

The milliasaur sprung. This was it. Point-blank. Point. Kill.

click

Misfire.

That was the last thought to scurry through my brain before the monster punched into my shoulder and slammed me back against a wall. I went down. Its writhing body fell on top. I had no escape, its spasms pummelled me, its rock-shard hide crushed my body and pierced my skin, its steaming hiss assaulted my ears. I protected myself as best I could. Screwed into a ball, battered by its throes, I cowered. Then, an unseen lightning-fast blow, my face exploded. My head bounced off a stone and I was plunged into oblivion.

I lay there. The dead weight of the milliasaur's corpse pressed down on me. I don't know how long it was, I'd lost track of time. To begin with I didn't even know it was dead, that my broken knife blade had torn open its throat as it had tried to swallow the pieces. I was just grateful that it had stopped; I didn't care why. I was lucky it hadn't collapsed on my chest or I wouldn't have been able to breathe. Instead it had finished up lying over my entire right side, literally pinning me to the ground with the sharp edges of its hide. I was bleeding underneath it, but the weight of the creature cut off my blood supply, like a tourniquet. First I felt the warm fluid cooling, then, as the minutes crawled by, it began to scrape away in clots on my fingers. The gritty residue got under my nails.

I had to move. Even if I wasn't too badly hurt, I needed a drink. My raging thirst had been made worse by the acidic taste of the blood I'd swallowed. An image resurfaced in my mind, of me, with a beautiful woman in one arm and a bottle of Wildsnake in the other. Well, there was no booze and the only thing in my arms was… well. My half-hearted laugh turned into a splutter, which devolved into a coughing fit, a painful coughing fit as every movement pulled at my limbs and dug the milliasaur's hide in a little more. I had to move. I figured what with a worm being basically one big cylinder it would be easiest to roll it off. Slowly I brought my free left leg up and around to get my foot against the corpse's side and squirmed my body to brace my shoulder against the wall; then I tried to move it. It was easier than I thought it would be. It had been its speed and power that had done the damage, not its weight. There wasn't much pain to begin with; everything was too numb. But when it rolled off my shoulder and thigh and flattened my hand I screamed myself hoarse as the rocks on its hide dug into healthy flesh. A swift kick fuelled by agony drove it off me completely as I yanked my injured hand clear. The limp tube flopped away.

You can't cut off the circulation to a limb without expecting some payback. I knew what was coming. With the arteries clear, the blood flooded back through my system. I rolled in torment on the rocky floor. I felt angry, angry that I had won. I had won, and all I got was pain and more pain. I knew this would pass, though. My real fear was that the scabs over my wounds would burst under the pressure and I'd start bleeding again. When it finally passed I struggled up against the wall, the wall that had kept me trapped against the dying milliasaur, so I was sitting upright. My arm was a mess, the dried blood had been scraped off in some places, leaving streaks of brown, alternating with skin either rubbed raw or bruised blue. My shoulder and elbow were sore, but I flexed my fingers fine. I couldn't see my leg through my trousers, but I guessed it looked pretty much the same.

Gingerly, I tried to get to my feet. I took it slow. I drew my left leg under me, then the right. I gasped, there was something wrong with that knee. Pushing myself up onto my hands, I tried to keep as much weight as possible off it. Then, leaning into the wall to balance myself, I got my left foot on the ground and stretched out that leg. My head swam and I fumbled for a firmer grip on the rock. Only then did I gently lower my battered right leg. It was stiff, and the knee hurt, but I figured if I kept it straight I could make it.

I limped over to the body of the milliasaur, I needed proof that I killed it and I was sure as hell that I wasn't going to drag the entire thing out of here. Something it couldn't live without, the old man had said. Now I'm no great student of worms, and I've heard stories of how you can cut them in half and make two of the monsters, but I know that in the vast majority of cases taking off the head is a pretty safe bet. It sounded simple when I thought of it, later I realised how difficult it was to carve through a neck made of rock with a few shards of a broken knife. But that thought would wait, because I'd just seen my gun.

It was hiding underneath the body, it must have been dragged down there by the worm when I kicked it off me. I felt sick, betrayed. A misfire. I didn't want to pick it up, but I had to, if for no other reason than that it had been entrusted to me and it had to be returned. I eased myself down and grasped it with my bloody fingers. Maybe I could fix it, for the journey back. I flipped the barrel open and six empty chambers stared back at me.

When I finally heaved myself out of the pit, the breeze cooled the sweat on my body. He was standing there looking for all the world as if he hadn't moved an inch. I thought I noticed something in his eyes when he saw me, a… softening, only for a second and then it vanished. Bruised, battered, blooded, with the face of a milliasaur strapped onto my belt. I must have been quite a sight. I limped towards him, my broken knife in one hand, the pistol in the other. Every single step back out I'd been thinking of what I would do. Should I get mad? Should I thank him? Or maybe act like I'd never noticed? I'd done what he asked, I'd got my trophy, I should just say what I was supposed to say, what he wanted me to say, and then I'd be in. I'd be one of the gang. But part of me wanted more, wanted to demand an answer, wanted to rip his head off. It drove me mad. The choices whirled round and round in my mind until I said to myself; no more, when I got there, when I could look in his eyes I would know what to do.

Now that time had come. I let the gun slip from my grasp; it thudded in the dirt. I wrenched the dripping trophy from my belt and dropped it on top. There. My victory, my knowledge, my question were plain for him to see. I waited for a flicker of response. There was none. His aged, bloodshot eyes returned my gaze impassively.

"Get it?"

The hard, metallic words whispered from his respirator. No praise. No apology. What little blood remained in me boiled. The fist came out of nowhere, I didn't even see it until his head slammed to the side. I couldn't believe what I'd done. I stared at my hand as if it were another's. I was shocked, but I felt good. He turned back to me, his respirator hung uselessly off the side of his face but his expression was the same. My pleasure turned to ashes. Had he even felt it? But then, there it was, a tiny drop of crimson emerged from the shadow of his nostril. It edged its way past his nose-ring and began the long journey down to his cracked lips. I smiled. I soared. He didn't even bother to wipe it off before he picked me up and drove me into the ground. Then he hauled me onto his shoulder and started back. His laughing made it a bumpy ride, and he didn't stop for long damn time.

Richard Williams

Whiskers on kittens

We fried ants under a magnifying glass. Just because it delighted us. Oh, they scuttled and ran away, but we caught them — pinning them down in a white dot of searing light that burst into a heat that exploded their little bodies. They made a tiny puff of smoke as they fell into ash, and we laughed.

When the bell rang, we'd throw the magnifying glass back to Winifred (it was hers — we'd stolen it) and scramble back into the classroom, dusting our skirts and picking bits of gravel out of our knees.

"I wish you wouldn't."

"Oh shut up."

Winifred had a dignified manner that annoyed us. We didn't know how to say that her restraint and calm common sense reminded us of our parents — so we didn't.

"Shut up."

"Shut it."

"I *said* —" at this point Winifred's eyes would tighten and her voice would become petulant, "I wish you wouldn't kill those ants."

"Winifred?"

"Yes?"

"Shut up — shut up — *shut up*."

She stuck out. She was different. She was too tall. Her name was too long — it made us laugh.

Winifred. Winnie. Winnie-the-pooh. Winnie-fred. Freddie. La la. Ha ha.

Her name stuck out beyond the Toms and Kates of the register just as her head appeared over the heads of her classmates in assembly. As if she had pushed and kicked her way up through a sea of bowl-cuts and pigtails and was desperately treading water, gasping for air.

There was a determined gracelessness about Winifred. She *tried* to get out of your way with the same quiet concentration with which she tackled everything. She never wanted to trip people up, and she never wanted to lose every race she ran. She never wanted to bump into people, or to step on their toes. But then she only ever once did anything completely, successfully and with such thoroughness that no one could doubt it. And that was inadvertent. I know it must have been.

I think she was in a hurry. One of those times when you fumble for the door with one hand, as you pick up your bag with the other, as you step into your shoes and run for it. That's how I imagine it.

She sat next to me for about four years — four whole years. Four children's years, too, when four years was the far side of forever: nearly half of my whole entire lifetime. But I never knew her. Not properly. I mean, there were moments — times when the cracks would show, and in the chinks you could get a glimpse of the kind of person that she would never allow herself to be. The kind of person that she would never have the chance to be. She had a quick lovely smile that would flicker across her serious face. It made her eyes shine like wet slate on a cold November beach.

She cared for things in a way that I didn't understand. I flitted; my mind bobbed and weaved and I scampered from thought to whim with barely a look back. Winifred *thought*. She remembered, and she followed things through. I thought that was Dead Weird. She would recognise kindness with considered and genuine gratitude.

"May I borrow your rubber?"
"Course — hereyar."
"Thank you. Thanks." In that small serious voice.
"Shut u-rp!"

We both attended Hillside Primary School, a dreary, tired looking building perched uncomfortably between the stony old houses of the village and a main road where cars and trucks wailed past at improbable speeds. The Primary School itself was tatty, the walls needed painting; the doors were scuffed at with years of football boot kicks, the classrooms were draughty and full of *real* 'desks': their tops heavy and shiny with years of golden-syrupy varnish, and with holes in the top in which you could put your ink pot. ("Ink pots?" we said, incredulously. "They used ink pots?" We didn't believe it. They were always lying to us.) The main gate did not open, had not opened for years, and remained rustily bolted shut while we trudged the long way into the building, past the fence and the blind corner where the squeal of car brakes howled through your ears and took your breath away.

But the school building retained a kind of dignity that I never even noticed until I was herded into the first of a series of Portacabins at the age of eleven, and tried to put my finger on what my new school lacked. It lacked… it lacked memories. It lacked distinction and the kind of faded glamour that I had never thought anything of. Hillside Primary School wore its decrepit buildings with something of the refined air of aristocracy fallen on hard times. Letting the servants go. Selling the outbuildings. Leather patches lovingly sewn on the elbows of bespoke tweed jackets. *We* were a motley crew of kids, with a house-key on a piece of string round most necks and a cheque from the absent father flipping onto the mat each month. But while the number of classes dwindled down to just two, and the small numbers of pupils threatened closure of the whole school, the buildings fantasised over better times: a make-believe idyll full of the apple-cheeked offspring of happy farmers, the 'ping' of a pen nib in a glass pot of ink, home-made sandwiches at lunchtime, and mother waiting at home with the dinner ready.

We had a motto carved in Latin above the door that was now all but hidden by layers of peeling lichen. No one knew what it said or what it might mean. If I stopped on the playground to blow hot breath onto my cold fingers through my gloves, I would look up sometimes and wonder what those words were. Maybe some fabulous secret! Perhaps directions to buried treasure! Or a magic word!

On my last day of Primary School, Winifred told me quietly that she had found out what it meant. She was staring up at the plaque, the thin grey clouds reflected in her glasses, and her eyes were dull.
"It's the Bible," she said, "*Suffer the little children to come unto me.*" She turned her head away from the harsh blue of the sky and looked down at her feet. There was something very like bitterness in her voice, "Haven't we suffered enough?"

A boy from my class was killed outside the old gates. It provoked a spate of road safety sessions from Mrs Robinson, our young teacher with an earnest breathless voice and too much pearly eye-shadow. It brought reporters from a local paper to our school gates (we laughed when they tugged at the rusty hinges). It brought huge shiny speed limit signs that the drivers would have had to slow down to read. It also left a gap in my class; an empty desk that I did not like to look at. One morning we trooped into the classroom and the desk had gone, and we said nothing, but we were all glad.

I was six when the accident happened. Young enough for it just to *happen*. I was told that I must be feeling sad, unhappy, confused and upset. I was told to talk to my Mum. I was given a letter to take home, a letter that got squashed up against an old apple core in the bottom of my school bag and fished out about a week later. We each went to see Mrs Robinson in turn, and I sat outside the classroom on a chair far too tall for my short legs, kicking my feet wildly. When my turn came, I went in and just shrugged at her. I noticed her eyes fill up with tears when she emptied his drawer and put his storybook in the bin. I knew that it was okay to be sad, and we could talk to anyone we wanted to, that we would all miss Kevin lots, but it was still okay to feel as though you might be forgetting him, and that he had gone somewhere — "we're not sure where, but he's happy now, and hedoesn'tfeelanypain." Mrs Robinson rushed this bit with reddened cheeks. I narrowed my eyes and suspected her of lying.

And I didn't really feel anything about it. It was *confusing*, for about a morning, in an odd, unsettling way that sat at the bottom of my stomach. But then… it was ten thirty and time for play… and then drawing, and after that home time. It was all part of an arrangement of events that happened just out of reach. Whispered words just out of earshot, discussions of which I only formed the outcome, an item placed on the sideboard just far enough back so that when I reached to grab it, I pushed it further away. It rained. The sun shone. A tiny boy named Kevin with smudged brown eyes and garden cane legs was trotting determinedly to school when a car took the corner too fast, ran up on the kerb and smashed him like an eggshell against the picket fence. He left a bloodstain shaped like an imaginary island on the wooden slats. Kevinland. Kevindom. Kevinnia.

It was two days before Kevin's mother fell against the dark stain, hammering on it and screaming in a cracked voice. She was led away and the fence was tactfully replaced. I watched her with wide nervous eyes for a second or two, and then dashed off to play stuck in the mud.

I ran after Kath. I wanted to be her friend. She was loud, and funny, with a devil-may-care attitude that was infectious. She was continually swamped in the clothes that her older sisters had handed down: synthetic school blouses with elbows as thin as tracing paper and the rolled up cuffs banging against her wrists in ungainly lumps of material, jumpers with tiny threads escaping from the hem at the bottom. Kath had bright ginger hair and a wicked, crackling smile. She habitually stood with her feet splayed apart as though to balance herself against an onslaught of… what? Attention? Trouble? She courted them both with such frenzied eagerness that I really think she couldn't tell them apart. *I* saw her face when Mrs Robinson got her up in front of the class to shout at her. All those eyes, all looking at her; Kath didn't just enjoy it, she *thrived* on it.

Kath regarded Winifred with a mixture of bemusement and something a little more vindictive than that. I don't think she meant to be cruel. She was simply genuinely perturbed by finding someone so different to herself. She would poke at her, and hit out at her, simply as a means of trying to get a response. It was Winifred's *fault*, really. It really was. If she'd screamed, or cried, or run away, or done *anything*, we would have all been horrified into stillness, and would have slunk off in ashamed silence. But she kept quiet.

Winifred. Winnie. Winnie the pooh. Freddie. Ha ha.

And as we pushed forward to torment her, Winifred's face turned to me with a look of deep betrayal that made me want to hurt her even more.

I didn't want to be singled out like that. Winifred just *kept* doing it. It was embarrassing. I even went back to her house once. Just the once. She invited me properly:

"Amy." She had been colouring in some shapes for Maths, but lifted her gaze from the page and dropped it heavily onto me, "Would you like to come round one night for tea this week?"

"Um. Alright."

"Which night would be most convenient?" I wanted to laugh, but she still had that gaze on me, and I squirmed under its weight.

"Um. Dunno. Tuesday? I'll check with my Mum."

"That would be lovely."

"'Salright. Yes. Thanks."

How could you ever think she meant to do it? Or even that she didn't care? She was so *careful*... in every sense. It was so obviously an accident. Anyone who ever met her would have known that.

Winifred's house.

Well, half-house. She lived in half of one of the farm cottages on the other side of the village with her Mum, her Nan and her cat. "*Mother*, *Grandmother*, and *Tibs* my kitten," Winifred gently corrected me.

"*Your* kitten?" I was derisory, no one my age owned

a pet. Not a real pet all of their very own.

"He's mine. I bought him. And I feed him." Winifred's calm tone didn't seem at all offended.

"Oh."

We walked out of school and took the unfamiliar left hand turn.

"Bye Amy!" No. Don't see me. Not now. "*Bye Amy!*" I ignored it again. This time it was even more insistent, "*Amy*! Byeeeee!" I stared at the tarmac and felt my face getting hot. I tugged uncomfortably at the strap of my school bag, caught Winifred's eye, and knew that she realised I was ashamed to be seen with her. I felt myself getting angry.

I dragged my heels most of the way there. ("*What* do you *do* with those shoes? *Look* at those heels! You must walk without lifting your feet *at all*!" my Mum would cry in tones of mock horror.) We waited for what seemed like hours until we could cross the road, then we traipsed down the footpath, left at the end, past the meadow and up the track to the old labourers' cottages. The houses were squashed and squat: grey stone dumplings with dormer windows protruding from the roofs like great eyes. They watched me accusingly as we went up the path, 'Is this your friend, Winifred?' I imagined them asking, and I wanted to shout 'NO!'.

My uneasiness grew as we let ourselves into a small, dark kitchen.

"Where's your Mum?"

"She works."

"Uh-huh. And your Gran?"

I was interrupted by a tiny mew from the corner of the room; Winifred's face lit up.

"Tibs!" she called, and then again, faster and brighter,

"Tibstibstibs!" She ran across the room and picked up the unwilling kitten, pressing its tiny body against her face. "*Look* at him! Isn't he just the most... isn't he just... oh *Tibs*!" She buried her nose affectionately in his short fur as he wriggled and thrashed.

Tibs was very much a kitten. Not even slightly a cat. Little and fragile, he didn't walk so much as *pad* from place to place with his insubstantial weight. He had big eyes of an mottled greenish colour that took up most of the room on his face, just enough space for a tiny pink nose and little mouth at the bottom. His whiskers seemed to fall off his cheeks as though there was just not enough room for them.

"What do you think, Amy?" She had tightened her grip just as it looked as though he was going to escape, and thrust the defenceless animal in my face. I moved my fingers slowly towards Tibs and then whipped them back as he tried to scratch them in skittish anger. I repeated the movement, and so did he, then I waved my fingers above his head and he flailed with his little paws, revealing pink pads under his tabby toes, and claws so tiny they seemed almost like a joke. I began to laugh, and so did Winifred. Her grip loosened and Tibs sprinted away to hide from his indignity under the cupboard.

Winifred and I continued to laugh, and I noticed that while she was laughing, it was as though the awful tension that she lugged about with her was lifted. She seemed lighter, seemed younger — almost as young as me.

And I almost realised why I hated her so much. It was because I really couldn't help liking her. I genuinely liked her. I liked her quiet manner and her considered approach. The way she spoke the truth and didn't mess around. I liked the way she looked when she laughed: she looked friendly. But what could I say? I was nine. I couldn't sit down and say,

"Winifred, I like you, but you make me feel guilty. You *embarrass* me, but — in a weird kind of way you make me want to look after you... because I know how easy it is to hurt you."

So I didn't say it.

"Shut up!"

Winifred stopped laughing abruptly. I shook my shoulders uneasily, I didn't even know why I'd said it, but it wouldn't be unsaid now.

"Could I have a drink? Or something?" Shocking, and now rude, too. I felt myself getting crosser.

"Yes, of course you can, Amy. What would you like?"

"Oh — anything. Whatever. I don't care." An uncomfortable silence for a moment. "Where's the loo?"

"It's upstairs, second door."

"Um. Thanks."

And I ran out of the room and up the stairs.

Once up on the first floor, everything seemed different. I stopped for a moment, trying to clear my head. It was cool and shady upstairs, the windows were covered with material that diffused the light, cast dark dusty shadows into corners, and smudged grey where there should have been bright light. Inside, everything was eerily quiet; outside I could hear the high-pitched shouts of children playing a game, but they seemed very far away.

A sound.

I stopped.

What — what was...?

I edged forward into the gloom and squinted into the darkness of one of the bedrooms.

"Winifred?"

A quavering whisper, like something floating out at me from another world... I couldn't be sure. I could still hear the children playing outside, their screams and shouts getting fainter. I moved forward again, tip-toeing through a doorway. What was that?

A dark shape on an armchair, turned away from me towards the window. I stepped again, the floorboard creaked.

"Winifred!"

The shape moved, and I saw the hazy shape of an old woman. It turned in the chair so it was facing me, and as my eyes adjusted to the darkness I saw it clearly: feather-wispy white hair, bagged skin with veins like dark snakes writhing under the surface, little watery pale eyes buried in wrinkles, tiny bird-like body encased in an old cotton night-dress.

I screamed.

It screamed, and for a moment we were both caught, rabbits in headlights, staring at each other, our thin voices cutting through the silence of the darkened room.

Then I ran. I thudded downstairs, stumbling and falling down the last few steps. I raced into the hall, fumbling for my bag. Where was it? *Where was it?* Upstairs, the screaming carried on, and Winifred came running gracelessly into the hall,

"Where did you go? Did you disturb her? You're not meant to wake her!"

I found I was crying now, hot tears that I couldn't

quite explain, "Where's my bag? Let me go, I want to go home!"

Winifred grabbed hold of me in a tight grasp, "No! Calm down! You're going to stay for dinner!" Tibs decided he did not like the noise, and streaked straight outside in a line of tabby fur.

"No! I'm not — I'm going — I *am!*"

I wrenched myself free from her grasp and tore out of the house, only settling down to a fitful trot once I reached the end of the track and was well past the meadow. I never went back.

I heard later that her grandmother was housebound. That Winifred looked after her while her Mum was at work. That they locked her in the house while they were both out. I realised later that Winifred must have hidden her from me. Must have been as ashamed of her grandmother as I was to be seen at the school gates with tall, ungainly, thoughtful Winifred.

We didn't ever talk about it. She never invited me again, but I think in a strange way, it made us closer. We were almost friends. We had an unspoken bond: something neither of us could define or discuss, but it was there.

There was a lot we didn't discuss.

I only heard about it by a coincidence. When I was in my teens, the vet from the next village was telling us horror stories about the worst things that happened to family pets, and remembered a terrible story that her predecessor used to relate at dinner parties. I had to imagine myself how it might have happened. I think she was just in a terrible rush. An awful, terrible hurry.

I think it must have happened a few weeks before an

Art lesson that I recall particularly vividly. Art meant acres of newspaper on the floor, which took time to lay out properly... especially if you had no particular desire to do the painting itself, and you just wanted to spend as little time as possible doing Maths. Every now and then a tabloid would sneak its way into the newspaper pile, and what we called 'naughty pictures' would be laid out alongside the foreign news and the travel section. The boys would snigger dutifully and half-heartedly, '*Nipples!*' and the girls would have to pretend not to be interested, until Mrs Robinson bustled up, pinker and shriller than ever, to whisk the offending pages away out of sight.

Winifred sat with her paints and her jar of water on the far side of the classroom from me, in complete silence, almost motionless except for her paintbrush, her tongue stuck out in concentration. I found her concentration oddly distracting, and tried to busy myself with painting a scene from a story we had recently been told. I depicted the people and background in blues, as there was not much of any other colour left in the paint pots nearest me. Mrs Robinson came round, making encouraging comments about every picture,

"Ah. Amy — very good. Nice colours... Kath — *do* sit down and finish your picture!... sorry, Amy. Blue is a very *sad* colour, isn't it?"

"Yes..." No. What *was* she talking about?

"You might want to make it a bit bigger... try to fill the whole sheet of paper, not just that one corner."

I obligingly splashed out across the sugar paper with an impetuous streak of green, and looked up expectantly. But I could see that wasn't what she'd had in mind.

"Ah, now, Winifred! Very good! Very good indeed!" I turned with jealous speed, to see Mrs Robinson holding up Winifred's painting, a laboriously painted picture of a small brown cat with grey-ish black tiger stripes, spindly long whiskers and big green eyes. "Look everybody, look at Winifred's picture."

Everyone turned towards it with grudging admiration. They all had their backs to me, and I called out piercingly, "It's *Tibs*, isn't it?"

"Is that his name?"

Winifred was too slow to reply, I called out again, "Yes, it is ...he's her kitten." I paused, while classmates looked at me curiously, ('*How does she know?*') and blundered on: I wanted to claim my share of it. "He's very sweet."

Winifred's face slowly broke into her beautiful smile, and Mrs Robinson put down the picture and had hugged Winifred before she remembered she wasn't supposed to. Had she never seen her smile before then?

Back in the classroom after playtime, Winifred was crying. Crying in a way you wouldn't think Winifred would be able to cry — crying in a way that was embarrassing to hear. Swollen eyes, harsh voice, red cheeks. I sneaked the room, pretending to go back for my coat... maybe by the time I came back it would have stopped.

"It's not, I *can't* — it's *ruined*! It's spoilt, it's *ruined*! ...It's all my fault!" she shouted, in between sobs, while Mrs Robinson soothed her with a calm flow words and tissues,

"Winifred, it doesn't matter, you can paint another picture, Winifred, you're very good at Art, we can rescue it, if we just paint over this bit here, of course it's not your fault, Winifred, someone horrible and vindictive has spoilt your picture because they were jealous, we can sort something out, we'll fix it, we'll look at it after school…"

"It's *ruined*!… and it's all my fault. I deserve it."

Beside them on the desk lay Winifred's picture, covered with blobs of red paint, through which Tibs seemed to be staring blankly like the corpse of an animal left by the side of the road. I think they had to throw it away, because every time Winifred saw it, her eyes would fill up with tears again.

I think she was caught off balance.

I imagine she was rushing to get to school, having made her sandwiches, and seen her Mum off to work, and made some lunch for her grandmother and left it on the table. Perhaps she realised she had forgotten her key and went running upstairs in her ungainly fashion, feet everywhere. Maybe she came back downstairs and turned too quickly…

I think she must have half-fallen, off-balance, caught herself just in time and thrown the whole of her nine-year-old weight onto one foot.

Oh, Winifred.

I doubt very much that she cried.

She would have stood quite still for a moment, maybe for longer. A quiet, still moment that was suspended, guilt-free, between two worlds. Then she would have removed her shoe without even looking at it and gone quietly to where she knew the carpet cleaner would be. (I must have been about fifteen before I knew such a thing existed.)

She would have been quite careful, and very thorough. Thorough enough not to allow herself even a single tear, even when her shoulders heaved as though her heart would break. No tears would have been her punishment to herself.

It would have been a sickening sound: a crunch, the crack of his little skull, a half mew and a worse silence.

Our vet friend said she thought it was "…carelessness, just plain *cruelty*, that's what makes me so cross and so very sad." And I wanted to shout at her, to ask her whether she'd ever been a child, and ever made a stupid, stupid mistake. I wanted to take her by the shoulders and shake her and tell her that carelessness *wasn't the same* as cruelty — it just wasn't the same at all.

Rachel Tripp

Rocketman

(Summer 1969)

Moon walking

My brother is in the back yard doing his impression of the astronauts walking on the moon: "That's one small step for man, one giant leap for mankind." He repeats this over and over: *one small step for man one giant leap for mankind one small step for man one giant leap for mankind* As he talks he jumps from one foot to the other, slowly slowly. Like he really is walking on the moon. Like he's one of those rocket men on TV, kicking up moon dust and talking to the President from a telephone in outer space. The night they landed my father came home early, and we all watched it live in the living room. Everybody sat still and quiet, even Minnie, and I saw Robin was thinking hard as he leaned forward into the blue flickering light.

the eagle has landed the eagle has landed the eagle has landed I drop my doll and start jumping around with him. There hasn't been any rain all summer and the yellow brown grass pricks my feet. *the eagle has landed the eagle has landed the eagle has landed* Just then the back door opens and my mother comes out. She has been cooking and there are stains on her apron. Robin doesn't notice she's standing there looking at us, until she yells at him to stop. *Robin! Robin, get your sister in here!* Robin stops pretending and turns right around to look at her. *Mission Control we have a problem.*

Cake

Our house is by the highway. Sometimes when I can't sleep I kneel by my bedroom window and count the cars that go driving by: big, shiny trucks going up and down, fathers on their way home after their late shift at work, sweethearts out for a drive. Next door there is a motel with a pool, and in the summer time, when it gets really hot, our mother takes us there. Because today is Robin's birthday she took him and some of the kids from his grade and the neighbourhood.

For his birthday, my parents gave Robin a new football. I know he really wanted one of those space ship models they sell at Simmers in town, but my father says it's time Robin started acting like other boys his age. He says that come the Fall he's sending Robin to the George Washington Military Academy. *Fourteen. You're not a baby anymore*

*   *   *

Everybody is back from the pool and hanging around the yard, waiting for the barbecue. My father is by the grill, getting the coals just right. He pokes at them with a stick until sparks leap up like fireflies, and the coals burn red red hot. He isn't wearing his cap and I can see the wetness on the part of his head where his hair is going. He says it is because we kids drive him so crazy that he is losing his hair. I am standing at the table with all the food on it. It's my job to make sure that Minnie doesn't jump up and lick the food the way she does sometimes when we are having dinner in the kitchen; and to give the grown-ups plates and knives and forks if they ask. My mother tells me I must smile and act like a lady. She says if I don't learn to be a lady, no man's ever going to want to marry me. I tell her I don't want to get married. But my mother says I will. She is laughing with the other mothers as they set up bottles of soda that hiss when you pop them open. She is wearing her red cotton dress and red lipstick and I watch as she lets out a laugh you can hear from the other side of the yard. When she laughs her lips part wide and her brown hair falls away from her face and she looks very pretty.

I'm waiting for her to notice that Robin's missing. He's been missing since they got back from the pool because he hates parties and being with kids who aren't even his friends. He hasn't got many friends, just me and Ed White. Ed White's a rocket man who died when his space ship blew up, but Robin says Ed still talks to him all the time.

My mother has gone inside to fetch the cake. It is chocolate with white frosting and Robin's name written on it in blue curly letters. When she is out of sight my father comes up next to me and stands close. *Where the hell's your brother. Go and find him before your mother gets back.* Over the fence I can hear the sound of the traffic as it speeds by.

Planetarium

Our father is taking our mother to the hospital to see her aunt who is sick. It is dark outside and Robin says the hospital called to say Aunt G is dying, and that's why they are going out this late. When the car has pulled down and out of the driveway, and we can't see the red of its taillights anymore, we climb up on to the roof of the garage. If it's a clear night Robin likes to sit up there and watch the sky, and sometimes I go with him. We climb up and lie on our backs with the dirt and the dead butterflies and look at the stars shining back at us like a thousand fairy lights strung up across the black. If Robin feels like it he tells me about them. Like how they've all got special names: the Big Dipper, the North Star, the Seven Sisters, the Bear. Or how in the old days sailors read them to find their way back home from the ocean. Robin knows historical stuff like that; he keeps it all in his head like a library. If you ask him he'll explain all about the Russians sending the first satellite into space, and how many dogs died before we managed to get one man on the moon.

Tonight though, all he wants to talk about are his dreams about being a rocket man. How when he grows up he's going to be one of those men at N.A.S.A and ride a rocket deep into space. *What does N.A.S.A stand for?* When he gets there he says he's going straight to the moon. Robin's just crazy about the moon, he's got pictures of it all over his bedroom walls which he gets from magazines he buys, and which the planetarium gave him that time he went for his science project. I ask him what he'll do when he gets there and he says he's got big plans. My brother's full of big plans. He tells everybody that he won't have to stay in this crummy town forever because when he gets to the moon he's building a city. A city on the moon. I try to imagine it white and shining. Whenever Robin talks about the moon, I look him straight in the eyes so he knows I'm listening, but my father's different. He says Robin's nuts. He says no fool is ever going to let Robin near his rocket, and even if some fool did, nothing can survive on the moon. Rock and ash that's all it is. *rock and ash rock and ash rock and ash.* Robin doesn't say anything when our father goes stepping on his dreams like that. He stays real quiet and writes in his notebook.

Ball

It's hot and sunny and I'm lying on the deck chair that's lost its cover. I'm wearing my yellow bathing suit and my legs and shoulders have started to tingle and turn pink. My father is in the yard with Robin. He's trying to teach him to play football but Robin isn't very good. I listen to my father's voice as he gives Robin orders: *Come on, not like that, like this.* He pretend-catches the ball to show Robin how to jump so he won't miss a high pass. *Got that?* My father asks. Robin doesn't say anything. He just rubs between his fingers, the way he does when he's feeling the butterflies.

When my father throws the ball he makes a little sound and I watch it spin through the air like a brown bullet until it hits Robin hard. Robin catches it but doesn't hold on. The ball slips from his fingers and bounces and rocks along the ground until it hits the fence and stops. *Fuuuummmmble* my father says like he's one of those sports reporters on the radio. Minnie comes over and jumps onto my lap. I put my hand on her soft fur and close my eyes and listen to the sound of kids splashing in the pool next door. They are laughing and screaming and I imagine I am one of them, holding my breath under the clear water. *You're gonna have to learn to play football if you're going to Fort Washington. They don't like pansies.*

*   *   *

It has cooled. The yard is getting full of shadows and soon the crickets will be out singing their scratchy song. When the hairs on my arms start to stand up, I push Minnie off, and get ready to go inside. With my fingertips I feel the bumps on the back of my legs that match the pattern on the chair. My father is still practising football with Robin. Robin's face is red with trying and he has hurt his knee. Later, when Robin and my father can't see to play anymore, my father will let Robin go inside too. From my room I will hear the sound of Robin's sneakers coming up the stairs, and then his door softly snapping shut.

Riding

Robin doesn't feel like talking. He's got what my mother calls the 'mean reds,' so I leave him alone thinking, and take my bike round to Ruby Glakey's house. Mr Glakey is a truck driver so most of the time he's on the road. My father says that it is probably Mrs Glakey who keeps him driving because she's always crying or hugging people. "A real piece of work," he calls her. My mother says nobody in the family has been the same since Ruby's brother went missing in Vietnam.

When I get to Ruby's house Mrs Glakey is outside digging up her flowerbeds. She is wearing a dress with orange patterns all over it and a straw hat and no shoes. When I come through the gate she looks up at me "Well, hi there Caroline, what a nice surprise. Come over here and give me a kiss." She puts her arms around me and squeezes so tight I think my heart's going to stop. "Ruby's upstairs. She'll be glad to see you."

Inside I find Ruby in her bedroom dancing to her sister's Chubby Checker records. When she sees me she stops what she's doing and shows me the new stuff her father has sent her from the road. Mr. Glakey is always sending Ruby and her sister stuff from the places he's been to. She's got caps and t-shirts and pins and stuffed bears with things like, "The Big Apple," and "The

Home of the Sweet Potato," written on them. This time Ruby shows me a T-shirt. It's light green with a big yellow sun on it, and at the bottom it's got written: "California, America's Sunshine State!" in black, cartoon letters. Ruby puts the T-shirt over what she's wearing. It comes right down to her knees and if you look quickly you think she's wearing the T-shirt and nothing else.

Ruby and me decide we'll go watch the cars on the highway so Mrs Glakey makes us sandwiches and puts them in paper bags with some cookies. We take our bikes and go sit on the walkway that runs over the top of the highway, and look at the cars as they drive past underneath. Whilst we are talking Ruby drops bits of chocolate chip onto the cars that zip under. She tells me about how her father says he's coming home for a few days and when he does he's going to take her to the new movie house that's opened up. Then she asks me if I want to come. I say sure and bite into my sandwich. Jelly oozes out of the sides and drops onto my shorts.

After we've watched the cars for a while and made up stories about whose driving them, Ruby stands up and starts to dance. She says she's going to be a famous dancer when she grows up and I tell her how I'm going to make dresses for rich ladies. Then Ruby says: "This is how my sister dances with her boyfriend." She turns her back to me and starts rubbing her hands up and down her sides. She looks like two people kissing and we laugh until our eyes get wet and our stomachs hurt.

Pool

My brother is playing dead. He lets his body float up and just hang in the water, head down, everything real still. Sometimes when our mother takes us to the pool, Robin lets me swim through his legs and make-believe

I'm a dolphin, but not today. Today he wants to play dead so I let him. I let him until he doesn't move at all, not even a tiny bit. Until I can't see those bubbles floating up around his head. Until I think he might really be dead. And then I get scared. I get scared and feel the way I did that time I got lost at the grocery store. When I get that feeling I start to kick the water. I kick and kick and kick as hard as I can, until Robin stops playing dead and tells me to quit it.

Dressing Up

My mother likes to dress up. She says she used to get dressed up all the time when she and my father first started dating because he would take her to all kinds of fancy places, even though he couldn't afford it. She says he would do it just to impress her because he thought she was classy and he wanted her to be his girl. She says he took her dancing or to the movies, and they would stay out late and grandpa would get mad. My mother and father never go out together anymore. My father says that he's too busy making ends meet. He says that when Robin and I get into the real world we'll understand what he's talking about. My mother still likes to dress up though. Sometimes if my father isn't coming home until real late, my mother clicks on the radio and gets dressed to go out. First she puts on her face, then her clothes. When she's looking all neat and pretty she takes herself to the movies. She likes the old ones. The ones with singing and dancing and beautiful women with perfect hair, and handsome men who always pull out chairs and open doors. When she's taking herself to the movies she drops Robin and me over at Ruby's, and Mrs Glakey gives us popcorn and lets us stay up as late as we want.

Snake

From my window I see Minnie arching her back at something in the yard so I go down to take a look. Lying there in the sunshine I see it, gold and black. At first I thinks it's a prank snake, like the ones the boys leave in the girls' locker room at school. Then after I've watched it for a long while I see it move. It rubs its belly in the dirt, just a little from side to side like it's getting comfortable. When I've seen it move I run to tell my mother that there's a snake in the yard, and she calls my father at work and tells him to come home right away. I don't think my father's gonna come because my mother starts to cry and says she can't just leave a snake in the yard when there's children to think about. When my father's car pulls up I can tell he's mad about having to come home in the day. He takes off his jacket and walks up to the shed at the back of the house without saying a word to me or my mother. He comes out holding the shovel he uses for digging and walks slowly up to the snake. It's still lying in the sunshine where I saw it and it doesn't move even when my father is close enough for his shadow to touch its body. Maybe it's dead now I say. No he tells me, it's just sleeping. Then he lifts the shovel up high and brings it down, quick on the snake's head. The snake leaps around in the dirt and my father brings the shovel down again and again until it stops leaping. When my father's sure the snake's dead, he picks it up with the shovel and throws it over the fence into the highway. Later, when my mother has gone inside, and my father is back at work, I go look at the blood patch on the ground. It's the colour of crushed black berries and with my foot I kick dirt over it until you can't see it anymore.

Going Away

On the morning Robin is going away, I wake up early and go downstairs in my pajamas to say goodbye. My father is driving him and he says he wants to hit the road before the traffic gets heavy. Robin's got a faraway look in his eyes as he stands with his suitcase, waiting for my father to unlock the trunk of the car. He is wearing his new blue and white uniform and his brown hair is cut short. Last night my mother helped him pack up the things he needed, and this morning she made him a baloney sandwich that she put in a bag with a quart of milk so he doesn't get hungry on his first day. She gives it to him as he stands in the driveway. Suddenly my throat gets all achey, like something's got stuck in it, and I start to cry. My mother comes over and puts her arms around me and tells me not to cry because Robin will soon be home for the holidays. She is wearing her robe wrapped tight around her and I put my hand in the pocket. When my father has finished putting Robin's things in the car he says they should go if they are to make it to where they're going by lunchtime. Robin doesn't take a look back as he's driving away, even though I'm waving like crazy.

After I can't see Robin or the car anymore I go to Robin's room. All his pictures are still there and his moon stuff because my father says Robin isn't allowed that kind of junk at his new school. Robin says if I break anything, he'll kick my butt when he comes home, so I don't touch anything. I just take a real good look and then leave, closing the door behind me.

Epilogue: the moon - a rocket man's guide to

The moon is dry and dusty and bare. There is no air

to breathe. It is very hot when the sun shines and very cold when it does not. Nothing lives there. Notable physical features include: Aristoteles Arzachel Atlas Autolycus Azoph Bally Ball Barrow Beaumont Bessarion Besel Biot But Blancarius Blanchinus Bond (w c) Bonpland Boscovich Brayley Bullialdus

The Sea of Tranquility: Latitude 0.6875 N
                              Longitude 23.43 E

Full moon occurs at the instant during the month when the earth is most nearly in line between the sun and the moon. At the instant of a full moon, a man on the moon and at the center of the moon's visible disk, would cast no shadow. In those months when the moon is closely enough in line north and south, an eclipse occurs. In astronomy the word eclipse means the obscuration of light of one celestial body by another. The two most familiar types of eclipse involve the sun, the earth and the moon, but equally well, one component of a double star may eclipse the other if their orbits are properly orientated relative to the earth R.D. Baldwin The University of Chicago. 1966

Dear Sir I am a boy of twelve years and would like to become a rocket man. How should I go about it? Robin Richards. M.I Ohio

N.A.S.A or the National Aeronautics and Space Administration has strict program for selecting its lunar astronauts. The initial measurable qualities demanded of candidates for astronaut training, by N.A.S.A.'s Manned Spacecraft Center in Houston are as follows: he must be a citizen of the United States of America; he must be an experienced test pilot with 1,5000 hours in jets, having attained experimental test flights in industry, N.A.S.A, or the military; he must be under thirty five years of age;

he must be under six feet in height; he must not mind: small spaces, darkness, isolation, the heat, the cold, silence, death.

Travelling time from planet Earth to the lunar surface: approximately 41 hrs. Cost of sending one man to the moon: approximately 4 billion dollars.

Facts: 1958 American government initiates plans to land a manned craft on the moon. April 12, 1962 VOSTOK I Soviet pilot Yuri Gagarin becomes first man to fly in space, orbiting the Earth once at 17,000 m.p.h, 200 miles up, for 89 minutes. June 3-7 1965, GEMINI 4, Jim McDivitt and Edward H. White Jr. orbit Earth for three days. During orbit Edward White becomes America's first space walker. January 27, 1967 APOLLO I., Virgil I. Grisson, Roger B. Chaffee and Edward H. White II killed by fire during routine pre-launch test. July 19, 1969 APOLLO XI 9.32 a.m. EDT KSL Florida Complex 39-A Neil Armstrong, Michael Collins and Edwin Aldrin Jr. lift off for lunar surface. July 20, 1969, 4.18 p.m. EDT Armstrong and Aldrin Jr. successfully land spacecraft in Sea of Tranquility. July 21, 1969 1.54 EDT lift off lunar surface for return flight. July 24, 1969 12.50 p.m. EDT crew splashdown in Pacific Ocean. Total duration of space expedition: 8 days, 3hrs 18 minutes. In that time an APOLLO XI astronaut will have: spent 21 hours 36 minutes on lunar surface; collected 15.9 pounds of samples; consumed 91.72 pounds of food; slept 32 hrs; grown 2 inches; prayed twice.

* * *

See the *rocket it is white it is bright. Come inside, hold on tight 10 9 8 7 6 5 4 3 2 1 Go. The rocket goes Up Up*

Up You go Up Up Up. Soon you will reach the moon and then this is what you will do. You will take a ride in a moon car, you will climb a moon mountain, you will live in a moon house. But first put on your space suit. Without it you can not live in the hot hot days. You can not live in the cold cold nights. You can not breathe the grey grey dust. So put on your space suit. Climb a moon mountain. Ride a moon car. Live in a moon house. Be a rocket man.

Meg Vandermerwe

Voices Are Different

The ground was waterlogged and I lay there still and silent through the night. Drizzle, which had fallen ceaselessly since the weekend, stopped at around six. The north wind that had accompanied the rain died off and by first light there was only an occasional drop, draining slowly from the ash and hazel branches overhead. My pulse increased a beat as darkness began to move and the fresh, clean air of dawn revealed the shining roofs of the town below.

Joe is asleep as they cross the border. The crossing no longer makes him nervous and he rests his head against the dirty-beige curtains by his seat. Sleep is his one sure way to stop thinking and he has become adept at dropping off at will — in armchairs, on train platforms, in cars. Though he never achieves full tiredness like he used to, he has trained himself to sleep fifteen, sometimes twenty hours a day. Even while awake he tries not to see. A green army kit-bag and a cardboard poster roll rest on the rack above. As the bus edges through Cavan and Meath he reads a book about football. The driver is tuned to a local station and whining country music drops down from muffled speakers. Across the aisle a young, unkempt student sprawls across her seat, a worn knapsack as pillow. She wears those maroon-coloured Doc Marten boots which Joe associates with college and which he has always disliked. Over her head like a hair band rest the headphones of a Walkman and try as he might Joe cannot pick up the music being listened to.

Through the city's outskirts he stares out the window at his own reflection, scarred by neon and darting car lights. In the bus depot, he observes the end of another day: blue-coated ladies sweeping chocolate wrappers and crisp papers before them. The huge timetable suspended from the ceiling is almost empty, the last bus of the day due at 11.15. Peter and David are over twenty-five minutes late.

Joe and Peter had become friends some years before. Pushed together by circumstance and slow to warm to each other, neither was much for words. Joe was the countryman and Peter the metropolitan: that was the game they played. Pinned to the wall in Peter's kitchen is a replica of an old map of Ireland, sixteenth-century maybe, the Pale coloured in light blue. Peter and his old school friends get together every New Year's Eve. Joe, although welcomed with sincerity, feels excluded from the start. He is not one of them, southern Protestants for the most part. There is one other outsider; he drinks tequila from a jam-jar. Conor is his name. Conor does not seem keen to talk though he rambles on briefly to David about some novel. Peter points to a press above the sink and Joe takes down the Beecham's, his head stuffed and neck aching.

Peter's house is nice; it is Joe's first time there. The ceilings are low. There is lots of wood and a strong smell of dogs. The long bus trip has made him tired and sweaty and he welcomes the hot pressure of the shower. As he opens the bottle of aftershave he thinks about her. The thick blue glass of the bottle distorts and discolours a mug of toothbrushes by the mirror. He had never been one for aftershave but she had talked about this brand once and some French soldier on a bus somewhere and how handsome he was and now that things have finished between them he has bought some as a sort of punishment. She had sprayed it on his hand once in a big department store and for the rest of the day she would lift the hand to her face. They had dinner that night. Joe has a photo. She wears a red dress. She smiles.

Rachel speaks to Joe through the thin polished oak

of the bathroom door. One of the school friends downstairs is having an asthma attack and Rachel needs a towel. He opens the door, smelling like the French soldier. She introduces herself, apologetic and smiling, takes a towel and leaves. Joe can hear the frantic coughing from below, temporarily crashing the party and forcing unasked-for sobriety. He looks at the steamed-up mirror. His body is thin and tired, his eyes swollen, bloodshot. Fragrance rising from hot skin makes him wince — red flashes darting through memory.

The area visible through my sight was small, ten yards across maybe, centred on a street corner. The birds had begun to sing though there was still only a thin veil of light. As a child, birds had been my passion, I liked the corncrake the best. In the book of birds I got for my tenth birthday it stands on a rock going crek-crek, crek-crek. Once my father and I were driving through mountainous country down in Mayo, not far from Lough Conn or maybe it was Lough Cullen, I'm never sure which is which. My father stopped the car suddenly. He thought he had seen something by the ditch. We got out and walked back the road. It was one of those July evenings when the air is rich and still, when night never comes. By the gable end of a ruined cottage on our right were some briars beside which walked a corncrake chick. Not many people have had that pleasure, to see a corncrake I mean. You've probably heard them if you're from my part of the world although each year they get scarcer. Nowadays when they cut silage they start on the outside of the field and as they move in the brooding hen is trapped. Her world disappears. But now December struggled on and Mayo and July seemed a long way off. A solitary blackbird was all I had, his sweet song filling the dark. Later there were others, a song thrush maybe though it could have been a redwing or a fieldfare come from Siberia. I know them all to see but voices are different.

The countdown to midnight brings a token effort to sing *Auld Lang Syne*. Three, two, one. The school friends hug and kiss, somebody flicks through the radio stations, Joe asks them to stop at the martial music. He hides from the school friends behind a glass of lemonade as the band plays *The Shores of Tripoli*. He doesn't know what to call how he feels then. Envy maybe and loneliness yet he doesn't want to be a school friend. Peter stands on the stairs and holds the asthma girl for a long time. Joe remembers. He thinks of her being held on a stairs somewhere by somebody who isn't him.

The glass shatters under his grip, a school friend turns and Joe signals that he is alright. Down on his knees, he picks each tiny shard from the smoothly tiled kitchen floor. Like diamonds they sparkle against the grainy blue of the tiles, their pretty lights a broken archipelago. A cut just below Joe's thumb drips red to the ground. As quietly as he can, he drops the fragments into a bin already overflowing with ash and lager cans and, turning to the sink, flushes out the wound, licking it until it is dry. He feels small and alone then against all this wood and these friends and in his head is a girl in a dress, her head resting in her hand. He wants her to be with him.

He goes upstairs to the room of Peter's parents. He closes the door behind him and sits on the bed, the thump of the music below pushing its way through floorboards and into the silent emptiness of the room. He looks at the jewellery of Peter's mother. A chain of pearls hangs from the side of a mirror, an aquamarine bracelet with matching ring rests on the sideboard beside a circular box with roses on it. He picks up the phone from the locker beside the bed and dials her number. It rings for a long time and with each ring his heartbeat increases. There is enough time for him to think about it all but he lets it continue and he has allowed his pulse to rise above a rate that is acceptable. A boyish voice answers. There is shouting and loud dance music in the background. He asks if he can speak to her and the voice says he will see and asks who this is. Joe gives him a name and waits. And now his breathing is raised and he feels the receiver slippy in his hand. The pearls seem for a moment to swing almost imperceptibly so that their image is captured by the mirror and Joe wonders where the draft is coming from. And for the first time he sees a photograph of Peter's parents, the two of them smiling, holding up salmon for the camera.

"Hello," she says, at the end of the line and her voice has not changed and she sounds happy, like somebody who could be your friend and he squeezes the receiver hard and hangs up.

Peter and Joe thrash dance. Joe screams out the lyrics. The room is cold, walls of glass and floor of stone. Conor sits passively, tequila-tired in the corner, while the music hurts their ears. The others are beyond, alternative entertainments imagined and traced.

8.43. To my front the sky is slate grey, behind me sky blue. I carefully lay the rifle down on the canvas bag and blow into my hands. Dawn has uncovered a blanket of webs spread silently across the earth. The dew has made me stiff and taut and I will not move again until the shot is off. The sounds of tractor engines and slamming car doors in the streets below have taken the place of my blackbird.

When, on the night things finished, she told him that it didn't feel the same, he cried. As the taxi pulled up and she prepared to leave his life with a relieved smile he whispered to the night. She was gone. Beneath the street lights the figures and letters of the registration plate grew dimmer. He stood motionless and wished he could be someone, somewhere else.

He had made no effort to socialise, clinging like a child to what he knew. He was glad for someone to initiate contact; Rachel was younger than Joe but seemed older, stronger. Each time someone had asked him that night what he was doing with his life it became harder to say, "Nothing." If only they could see. See that this was not him, that he was somebody, that there were other times and other places before all of this. But he could not see it himself and 'nothing' was all there was to say now. He wanted to shout, to be heard above the words of love, reflection and prophecy on this New Year's Eve. He wanted to look at Rachel and tell her the truth but instead he cowered, massaging his forehead, babbling about fulfilment. In his mind he sees a red dress and there is nowhere to hide in a Wicklow farmhouse amongst these friends of his friend.

Now I am in an Armagh hedge and I see the young soldier chewing. His eyes are tinged red but his jaw is shaven clean.

Conor puts a song on the stereo called *Bad Penny* and talks about a film where a bad cop meets Jesus. Joe asks Conor what he would do if he met Jesus on the way home. Conor does not answer but instead tells Joe about this film. The cop doesn't cry or he doesn't pray. He doesn't do what you expect. He is angry and he says to Jesus, "Where the fuck were you?" Imagine.

I know he is dead before I squeeze the trigger. Behind me in the high, bare trees the rooks scatter into the morning. Rooks are like blackbirds that way, you're always sure.

Frank Shovlin

Livelihood

I confess it. You all adore me for my contribution to science, ask me onto talk shows, buy my books hungrily. And yet for the past twelve years I've been hiding more knowledge than I have revealed. Contributing to science? I've been trying to strangle it. I could change the world should I care to, change it beyond all recognition. But then, I do not care to. I have renounced my own apotheosis, so why should I concern myself with yours?

Yes, I'm proud. I have a lot to be proud of. Proud I've borne my secret for twelve years. Even now, once I've unburdened myself to the deaf page I shall commit these words to the chimney's discretion; and then go on, as I have had to, in silence. I need not keep my secret much longer. I am becoming old now, and soon my secret shall be kept for me.

Proud, too, of my intellect. Over forty years ago I began my career in science with a First in Biochemistry from Durham University. It will upset many to know that I hated it there; those of my acquaintance were either stupid or dull. While I was there, though, I was witness to two of their deaths, both by misadventure of various sorts, which affected me deeply. The thought of simple ending. Ending with no great cause upheld, no reason save that death is easy and to live is irregular. It affected me, as I say, deeply, which will no doubt surprise you if you have put up with me this long, particularly given my gentle loathing of all Durham's inhabitants. But I am tender at heart, and attach great value to people, even those that nauseate me. After all, they are the same stuff as I am.

Aye, and there's the rub. It struck me as a bitter truth that every day brought mortality, and that the only option to awaiting its arrival was to anticipate the event.

Well, I was hardly going to settle for that, now was I?

Certainly not. So I took to postgraduate studies and accumulated, more or less by-the-by, a Master's degree, a doctorate, and a professorship in Cambridge, a place that suited me far better — full of driven people, as I was. And in my studies I began by availing myself of the still-new science of genetics. In this new field it appeared there might lie the key to understanding why the body will of itself fail after a while; and, once understood, might be reversed.

A naïve expectation, of course, and my studies soon branched out into ever more exotic and arcane directions, as I discovered new factors that constantly had to be woven into the problem of mortality. Virtually any factor you care to take into account will lead, ultimately, to dissolution. Unexpected phenomena such as gravity; the act of breathing, as much as not; and above all entropy. Our every action, our environment, the very laws of the material universe, all colluded in our execution.

But if I could put off death, that was something. If I could protect myself — and, by extension, others — from illnesses, petty accidents, the results of unhealthy living, then it would be a not inconsiderable achievement and one which I was confident could be achieved. Possibly such a process of change as I envisaged would never become a general phenomenon, but I was happy that I could so improve my body's auto-repair systems and perfect its defences from disease, and that would be enough for now. I would cease to age after the treatment and might reasonably expect to live, what, five hundred years or so longer; by which time no doubt I would have had time to develop my art and extend my lifespan still further.

In the meantime I was publishing a little of what I learned. Had no choice in the matter, had to keep the University happy with their pet biochemist. They liked the gist of my studies, felt that my reaching into mortality brought them kudos. Well, I allowed them to think so, just as long as it brought me the liberty to pursue my studies. And they were my studies, I can assure you. Nobody knew more than a little of what I learned, not even those I suffered to work with me. I selected assistants with great care. I wanted those who were bright enough to carry out my admittedly rough-and-ready orders, but not so much so that they could pierce themselves the mystery of the results that spoke to me directly. All along it was my project, my obsession. To have to share information seemed to me to demean it. And so I went on for twenty-eight years.

I was in my early forties when the change came. I had had one of my disastrous affairs with a pretty, stupid graduate. It hadn't turned out well, of course. As ever, she had demanded affection and attention on a scale I could not divert from my real passion — and in any case, I always suspect that they only desire me for my authority. On this occasion, however, the girl had actually had the gall to drop me! I was consequently in a late-November coffee-shop of the type that are increasingly mushrooming in academic areas, and I was brooding upon the deepening lines in a harsh face that sat in a mirror opposite me. There, it seemed, lay the crux of the matter.

The harsh face was joined in its reflection by a chest which, underneath some fashionable cloth, was finely-sculpted. A light and summer voice asked,

"Doctor Ballow? May I have a word with you?"

I looked up into the deeply-tanned face of a woman perhaps in her late twenties and the thought of the ageing properties of the sun flicked through the back of my mind. However, she had phenomenal eyes, so deeply blue they were almost indigo. But perhaps more shocking was the long braid of silver-grey hair, which seemed natural on an octogenarian, save for the style. All in all her appearance was remarkable, but undoubtedly attractive.

I reflected sourly that she was probably a friend of my latest romantic failure. The chances were good that I would hear from this stranger the usual platitudes that are hacked up by those whose concern is purely tangential; for which I had little time. However, in view of her desirability I grunted and motioned for her to sit.

Despite myself, I was impressed. As was usual at such times, she was nervous. I could see the words being marshalled behind her face, selected as she searched for an opening into her doubtless vitally important message. Of course she was nervous about approaching her friend's superior, they always are, and the usual few seconds of silence followed. But in all that time she held my gaze, kept her eyes from dropping, and I recognised the daring it took with approval. It made a change from nervously playing with hair or fumbling a cigarette.

I am not an utter monster. "Well?" I prompted.

"Doctor Ballow, how old do you think I am?"

This was very forward of the little minx, I thought. Nevertheless, I am rarely wrong-footed and went along with her for now, until I could discern some point to the conversation.

"Twenty-eight."

She shook her head. "I can remember," — her forehead wrinkled with concentration — "the building of the first pyramid at Saqqara."

"Goodbye," I replied, finishing my coffee and making as if to go. I have no time for fools, and will not tolerate my time being wasted in particular by young fools.

She leapt up. "No, wait," and tried to hold me where I was. Her hands were icy though my clothes as she barred my way.

"Do you feel how cold my hands are? Watch this. Sorry," she added, stealing a fresh cappuccino from a passing student. I took advantage of this diversion to push past her and out into the orange-black glow of early evening streetlamps. As I reached my car she dashed up to me, but I simply kept my back to her as I struggled with my keys. Some people simply cannot take rejection, I reflected with a smile of self-mockery.

"Now look," she said, and it was only when something heavy fragmented by my feet that I turned, furious that I should be assaulted in such a manner by an infantile loon. I was about to shout at her, push her away perhaps, but she was staring at the pavement with such intensity that my eyes followed hers down. The pavement was littered with shards of cappuccino. Coffee turned to ice, now glistening faintly in the lamplight. I crouched, picked up a piece, tentatively licked the clean side. Ice. Caffeinated ice. I glanced up, unsure what to make of the situation.

"It's to do with ageing," the grey-haired youth asserted. "The cold is something to do with ageing. I need your advice."

She had it. I drove her to my lab, though, and made her repeat her trick in test conditions. Fifty times. I watched her perform her trick fifty times, simply holding the beaker to freeze the water inside; timed it each time; varied the water temperature. Then I made her alter a thermometer reading by holding it, made her tremble with the effort as she strained to bring the temperature down still lower. At last I was prepared to grant that she appeared to suck a certain amount of heat from items she touched, and that this could be, to an extent, varied according to will. Only with this firmly established did I allow Ayshe to tell her story and finally try to support her outrageous claim.

I will not pretend that I did not enjoy Ayshe's tales about her life, such as she cared to tell me at that first interview. She had a habit of slipping into an unfamiliar accent whenever she reached particularly animated points in her narrative, and it was something that I learned to listen out for. She was a natural storyteller and over the course of the next few hours I was highly entertained. Not that I believed a word of it for the time being. The long and the short of it was, however, that Ayshe was uncertain how she had come into being, but for as long as she could remember she had never been hungry and had sucked heat from her surroundings. And she had not aged in four millennia.

How could I not be excited? This was possibly the greatest breakthrough of my career, the key to my quest , and it had simply walked up to me. Remarkable — as long as it were true. I admit, I acted the tyrant to make her prove her claim. I acknowledged that she could chill — but to go without food? It seemed preposterous. However, she simply offered to remain inside my lab for thirty days without sustenance. It seemed to be foolish; if she grew dehydrated or even died as a result of undergoing such a stupid test, then there would probably be trouble. The university was extremely understanding toward the behaviour of its finest scientist, but there were limits, after all. Still, no better suggestion presented itself immediately, so instead I sought to overcome any objections to the problem.

The laboratory was converted into a makeshift bedsit. A camp bed was set up, I found a few books, some paper, a radio and stole a guitar from an undergraduate. She couldn't play. I told her it would amuse her to learn. And then I simply set up a few video cameras in the room, so that she would be under constant supervision, weighed her, and left. I locked the door behind me.

I had the video cameras linked up to a monitor next

door, and over the next month that became my own dwelling-place. I would sit, watch the monitor or hurry through recordings of what I had missed; all the time the curious nature of her state was gnawing at me. There was no way she could be so old. Even were we to grant her claim to a certain age, still surely entropy would have eroded her by now, breaking down the order within her very cells. But sometimes I simply watched the screen.

She was not a lady of regular habits. Sometimes she would wash, using the laboratory sinks. It must have been the first time they had seen shampoo. Not that it seemed to make a difference, mind you. I never saw her clean her teeth. She claimed she never had done, but I didn't believe that and had bought her one anyway. She used it to smear long-forgotten chewing gum over the underside of the workbench where it lurked. She had a very brief concentration-span. She fiddled with the guitar for a short while, then abandoned it. Sometimes she sang strange songs which grated on my ears at first, until I accustomed myself to the mystery of its own idiosyncratic harmonies and tones. But very often she would try to draw for me the places and events she had described in her story; her hand was not as good at description as her tongue, though, and all too often I would see her tear up the labour of a morning in disgust.

Throughout the whole of her time I had her weigh herself, morning and evening. Every day it was the same result. It was not until after the experiment was over, though, and she stepped out of the laboratory as radiant as when she entered that I began to suspect what time would prove. There was, in the room, only a smell of ink; there was none of the stink one might expect of a lab inhabited for thirty days. Heaven knows, I've had it reek after a few hours of undergraduate occupation. So I followed this up. On the books, the pens, the toothbrush — no fingerprints. No fingerprints in the room that I had not deposited myself. Not one fine grey hair left anywhere. I knew then I had the answer.

Ayshe's body was a closed system. She had no need of sustenance because she was losing no substance; and the energy to maintain this system against entropy was provided by the universe itself.

I was staggered. If this hypothesis was correct, then I had been following the wrong track for decades — or rather, had been aslant the right track. It seemed so simple, but I had been blinded by a desire to eradicate the influence of any destructive forces. It had not occurred to me that radiation, in a very specific situation, could be beneficial. Of course I jumped at the opportunity to follow this up and begged Ayshe to let me perform further experiments. She was as keen as I was to understand her condition, indeed it had led to her search for me when she had come to hear of my reputation, and so I had a willing subject for my enquiries.

It took about a year before I could satisfy myself of the basic truth of my hypothesis. It had proved extremely difficult to get decent results with Ayshe. We tried to x-ray her, but the rays were absorbed absolutely into the girl. Scans of any sort were miserable failures. I experimented with the problem of why she breathed; but there were always problems, and after Ayshe stayed underwater for four hours with no ill effects I simply concluded that the main effect of breath appeared to be to facilitate speech. We tried to take blood samples: a very difficult procedure. It was possible to pierce her skin, but it was like driving the needle through a rock. Ayshe cried, ate a little, and went to sleep. When she awoke, she weighed the same as she had always done. To the milligram.

It was mostly with the blood, and a few laboriously-obtained tissue samples, that I tried to unravel the mystery of how she should have been created as she was. In the years of my research Ayshe was with me constantly. Her knowledge of science was pitiful, and her intelligence not entirely of the best, so she studied in order to understand herself, while I slowly discovered worlds inside her cells. She was of infinite patience; but sometimes, in the five years I used her for my research, she seemed to be in a kind of mental agony that I had always felt to be my own particular prerogative. And it moved me, in a way that no-one has done either before or since. For with Ayshe, unlike any other woman, there was no conflict of interest. She was my study, I was attentive to her minutely, on a scale I doubt has ever been echoed either before or since. To give her of my time was my duty and, increasingly, my personal inclination.

It was a single day that was to wipe all that out. Ayshe had taken early on to living with me, and so it was that I was roused one still-dark morning from where I had slumped in sleep over my desk. The house was reverberating to her screams; wild, primal shrieks, no humanity to them. I leapt up, ran to her room, but by that time all was silence. She lay splayed face-down, as if dead, upon her bed. The sheets lay scattered over the floor. I stood in the doorway for a long while immobile; then hurried to the bed, to persuade myself of Ayshe's wellbeing. At my touch upon her chilly back she stirred slightly.

"I can't cry," she whimpered.

"Of course not," I soothed, "Of course not, silly. You're a closed system."

She rolled onto her side and looked at me. This girl, this beautiful young old woman, lay naked opposite me. But there was infinite pain in her indigo eyes that put any lust I might have had to flight.

"I don't want to be a closed system, Gerald," she said. It sounded like a demand. I couldn't understand this at first, just stared in silence at the miracle that wanted to deny itself. "Help me. There's something wrong with me. Help me, Gerald, help me!" She was overcome with a fury I had Gerald never seen save me before and she was please please oh Gerald clutching my head help me with hands of ice I need help so I tore myself from her. I fought my way free, as she fell to clawing at her unmarked face and howling demands that she be let cry.

Later that day she sat me down, calmer now, to explain her behaviour.

"Gerald, I've lived so long now. There's nothing left of where I came from. All my friends from the start are long dead, and their children populate half the Earth. I've seen so many loved ones die. For so long I've not let myself love. I've had no friends, no place."

I would have interrupted here, moved to reassure her, but she smiled and waved my protests into silence.

"You're so sweet and loving, Gerald. But you'll only live so long, then it's back to loneliness again. Sometimes I just wish there were people who can really understand, who were there. I long just to talk about the Stylites in the desert, or the court of the Mahdi, or the dirty village that was once Rome. But nobody really knows, they can only listen and imagine what is worlds away from them. In my whole lifetime I have never met anyone like me. I'm the only one."

I broke in here. "But that's where I can change that! I've learnt so much, Ayshe, it's just a matter of time. Ten more years and I can replicate your condition myself."

She laughed then, and it cradled hysteria. "And then what? Oh, Gerald, don't be cross. But do you really want to see Britain submerged? To see the human race evolve, or die? The sun burn out? You may say so now, but no, not even with me. And that is exactly what I'm facing, and I want to die before I see all that come to pass, while you are here to be with me. While I can die beloved. I need your help, Gerald."

For some reason, the part of myself which held my emotions closed down, just at the time when perhaps I would be most ruled by it. Coolly, analytically, I looked at the problem. The only option, as far as I could see, was to stop Ayshe's ability to maintain herself against age and entropy. This could not be done; it was a natural function of her being. But she could be shielded from energy to do so. No heat, no radiation — or as near to none as possible, so long as her body could not maintain itself. She would simply corrode. In the dark and cold. Alone.

I tried to deny knowledge of how she might die, but she must have read it in my face, and she insisted I tell her, grew hysterical, badgered me till I hit her. And this set the pattern for the next six months. I was the keeper of the only thing she cared to know, and every day she would pray for death. And every day for six months I beat her into silence, thrashing her more and more cruelly. Maybe it was because she never marked, never reddened, never showed the signs of the pain I was inflicting upon her. I think I came to hate her for wanting to die when all I wanted was to live, and with her. She had become the very spectre of death's insistence I had tried to flee all my adulthood. Finally I raped her, brutally pushing into her while I tried to strangle the bitch.

In the quiet after that, when we lay panting and agonised on the floor in our worlds of misery, I realised the truth of what we had become. And so I told her how to die, quietly, and put the resources of my laboratory at her disposal. And in a silence almost surreal she turned to me, kissed me with cold lips and told me her love. She has eloquence, and can speak to stir a magistrate. I wept, there on the floor, and she cradled me in stone-cold arms and licked my tears away.

She constructed a sarcophagus. On my research budget she bought the stone, had it shaped and polished. Then, with her own hands she coated it in different materials until it was as radiation-proof as man could contrive. I let her do it, but it was a slow agony for me to watch her steady diligence in the fashioning of such a thing. I had no part in it. This was her destiny. But I helped her on the technical side — it was that or have someone else interfere with my beloved's death. So together, when Ayshe thought it done, we tested how much energy was penetrating the stone. Too much; but that was mostly heat. If it were below freezing point, then it would suffice. It should have been black. The stone was black. But the layers above reflected the sunlight away, and made it shine like a giant silver bullet.

Ayshe picked the spot for her interment. With the remaining money in my budget she had us flown, with the sarcophagus, to Switzerland. She wanted to lie inside a glacier, and had a helicopter transport her on her last journey, to the high ice-fields of the Alps. It left us by the side of a shallow crevasse, deposited the sarcophagus inside. A rill of meltwater pooled behind it. Finally, the country was empty, of noise, of time, of life. A strong shaft of sunlight caught her silver-grey hair.

In the high Alps of Switzerland lies a body, five-foot-six and deeply tanned. In the atmosphere there it is probably tautened and solid, human no more. This was my ambition, this my purpose, and now it is ended.

Alex Lawrence

Tango

Benjamin Faulks started taking Tango lessons at the advice of his doctor. "Go dancing, Ben," said Dr. Wordsworth one clear and breezy morning as Benjamin was buttoning his shirt. "It'll do you good".

Dr. Wordsworth was well-known for his sharp, unequivocal diagnoses, as well as for his up-front, almost crude manner. For him, things always had an explanation, and always made sense. Benjamin, on the other hand, had considered himself a man of letters (a term he preferred over the plain 'Lecturer in Modern Literature'). Often comforted by the cloudy distance from his subject-matter, by the evasive, non-committing solutions that had come to his mind, he had resented Dr. Wordsworth at first. But then he blandly accepted his physician's mannerism, and finally, to his own surprise, Benjamin had grown to envy him for that simple, non-fussy outlook on life.

"Dancing..??" Benjamin was utterly surprised. During his wife's long illness, and especially when her end was at sight, Dr. Wordsworth had come up with slightly unusual suggestions, "Just to make life a little nicer." And so, at his word, they both went punting twice a week, always equipped with a bottle of Cordon Rouge and a pack of strawberries, went horse-back riding, learned how to play golf and took up Shiatsu. Fortunately, that summer was brighter and sunnier than usual. It seemed longer, too, with its slow and unreal pace, but ended abruptly when Calista died, closing her eyes on the reddening ivies.

Benjamin had expected her death, had taken care to prepare himself for it, but he had never imagined how hopeless and hollow life would feel from then on. Waking up in a cold bed, cooking for one, coming back to a dark house. Losing weight, letting the hair overgrow. The dark circles around puffy eyes. The inability to smile wholeheartedly. 'Oh God,' he thought one day as Hilary term was approaching, 'I could never make it. Never would I be able to return to life'. That was when he rang Dr. Wordsworth again.

"Good to hear from you, Ben, how have you been?" For some reason, he insisted on calling him 'Ben.' Nobody else did, and he himself certainly did not conceive himself fit for the young, bouncy, sharp and energetic sound of that name.

"Not too bad, Doctor, not too bad indeed." Calista would have sneered at him shamelessly. What a lie.

"As it happens," said the doctor sharply, "I do not believe you."

Benjamin was dumbfounded. On second thought, this was easier than spelling it out himself.

"Ahhh..." he fumbled for the right word. He had respect for words.

"Are you eating well? Steaks, toffee puddings, Guinness?"

It has been long since Benjamin had enjoyed the creamy, bitter froth on his lips. Dr. Wordsworth continued, uninterrupted. "Righty-O, old chap, time for a pint. I'll meet you at the Mitre shortly after seven. Cheers." Then he hung up.

Benjamin sighed and put down the receiver. A pint. At the pub. Oh God.

The Mitre was warm and smoky. The soft carpet had swallowed his steps as he spotted Wordsworth leaning on the bar and chatting with the young man pouring his pint.

"No Guinness here, go for the Murphy's," he said as Benjamin unwrapped his scarf and unbuttoned his coat. They sat at a corner table.

"So," said Wordsworth, examining his patient's pale

complexion with interest.

"So," replied Benjamin, with a weary smile.

"You miss her terribly, don't you," shot the physician. Benjamin trembled with sorrow.

"I do," he said. "I keep hearing her voice all the time. It is as if she's still around, watching me, commenting upon things."

"Then surely, she would have told you to go for a pint a long time ago, not to mention the steaks."

"Calista did not approve of British Beef," said Ben, and broke into laughter for the first time since his wife had died.

The thing that scared him most, he told Dr. Wordsworth as their sessions proceeded, was the frosty glass wall that had formed around his mind and pierced his soul. He hadn't been much of a socialiser as it was, but now he had to summon all his powers, or what was left of them, to go through the drinks-parties and freshly-attended seminars.

"Hard thing to go through them even when you're in good form," said the doctor. "I avoid them whenever I can. 'Urgent call to the Operation Theatre.'" Even the need to nod to the occasional student on the street had clutched his shoulders like a heavy satchel, he said. Dr. Wordsworth had booked him a Shiatsu appointment.

But as the evenings grew longer, the days colder, Benjamin's recovery took a slow pace. He wished, at times, that his tormented mind would cease to be, or leave him in peace. 'Really, Faulks,' he thought to himself with Calista's Greek rolling r's, '*Ela*. Go get a life. You're losing it.'

Then came the palpitations. Just like that, one morning while delivering a lecture on Marquez in Schools, his heart was pierced and as if charged with a ticking time-bomb. He didn't stop, partly because he could not spare the attention, partly because his Oxonian etiquette had ruled this out under any circumstances. By five to eleven, his hands were shaking visibly, his knees were soft, and his voice had barely managed not to be choked by an unfamiliar lump in his throat. He had dismissed the class and made his way to his rooms as quickly as he could. Half way down Merton Street, as he nearly slipped down the pavement covered with sleet and rotting leaves, he changed his course and headed straight into Dr. Wordsworth's clinic.

"That was brave of you, Ben," said the doctor with bemusement as he shut the white door behind his trembling patient. "You could have been spotted by a student, you know."

"For Christ's sake, Wordsworth, I am not quite well." That, for Benjamin, was a grave understatement. He was almost drowned in his fear, and the rational attempts at understanding what befell him had blinded him with their lucidity.

The medical examination did not take long. Being a silent spectator for such a long time, and then a subject himself, Benjamin thought he would be indifferent to measuring blood-pressure, the burning chill of the stethoscope, the pinch of the needle under his skin, the blinding light in his eyes. But Dr. Wordsworth's silence was unusual, and upsetting.

"That'll do, Ben," he said as the Christ Church bell struck twelve. "Go get dressed."

Benjamin stayed put, the pale sunlight reflected on his white skin.

"Is anything seriously wrong?" he asked. He was not afraid, the worse was already far behind him, but he needed to know. He examined his physician closely, inquisitively, studying his movements, from the decisive tilt of the hand as he shook the blood ampola, to the scarcely-visible tightening of the lips. He was hoping to disclose some information.

"Go on, Faulks, button your bloody shirt, you'll catch pneumonia on top of that depression of yours."

Benjamin sighed with resignation. Depression. Clinical depression.

"So do I get prozac?" he asked in a matter-of-fact voice. The doctor looked at him with what seemed like a genuinely affectionate gaze.

"The high pulse rate, the weak knees, the irritability, topped with the fact that you still don't take to steak and chips, all point to that direction. Plus, that lump in your throat. I'll have to send you off to do some scanning, just to be on the safe side, but frankly I don't think it is necessary. What you have is called *Globus Hystericus*. It is a psychosomatic condition triggered by acute vulnerability in the Fifth Emotional Centre of the body. It has to do with a lack of will to promote one's vital interests, with inability to communicate properly."

Globus Hystericus. Ben couldn't help it. He started laughing.

"That definitely sums it up properly," he said with tearing eyes after a while. "So what do I do with it?"

"Go dancing, Ben. It'll do you good."

"Dancing…?"

"Dancing. Waltz, Salsa, Tango. Good fun," said the doctor, and saw Benjamin to the door. "Let me know how it goes," he added, and watched his patient walk slowly up King Edward Street and disappear in the High Street crowd.

Benjamin was no longer surprised by his doctor's creative ideas, but this time, for some reason, he had found it difficult to swallow. He did not question Wordsworth's goodwill, but dancing…? How could he dance with this long, awkward stride, the ridiculously-adolescent stooping posture and above all, his bloody introverted nature?

Nevertheless, and due to the doctor's persistent

calls, he had summoned his courage one Wednesday evening and cycled to St. Hugh's College, where the Alternative Latin classes took place. Walking through the carpeted corridor he still hoped that he could escape at the last moment, that the class would be cancelled, or overbooked. 'Really, Faulkes,' echoed Calista's voice, 'You act like a teenager facing his first date!' 'You are right as always, *Agapiti* Calista,' he sighed.

The hall was heated and smelled of wood and warm dust. It was empty. 'I might have got the wrong day, or time,' he thought. He didn't like being alone in a large room. Faint fumes from the kitchen slowly seeped into the hall, mixed with the muffled voices of hungry students.

"Must be tuna cannelloni tonight," said a soft voice behind him. Benjamin turned around, slightly startled by the presence of another person whom he hadn't noticed coming in. What he saw was the smile of a young woman.

"Ahh, yes, I believe so," he replied, and could not decide whether he was enchanted or threatened by her intuitive kindness.

"New here, I presume," she said. "Welcome, it's always nice to have more people around."

"Yes, thank you." His detached academic manner still resisted her warmth.

The young woman dropped her rucksack and heavy coat on the floor.

"Oh, don't do that, it will catch dust," he suddenly said.

"Don't worry, these have been around in worse places," she smiled, took her boots off and changed into high-heeled dancing shoes.

Benjamin had never seen such shoes. They were almost ridiculous in their golden colour and sparkling beads. But as she got up and walked around, stretching her long legs and arms, he saw the grace, the swiftness and the glamour. She was young, but not as childish-looking as some of his undergraduate female students. 'Twenty-five, I should think, and definitely not English,' smiled Calista in his thoughts. He watched her dancing in the quiet, empty hall to the music in her head. She was independent, peaceful and content in her dance. It was almost as natural for her as walking.

"That was beautiful," he said as she stopped.

"Oh, that's nothing, simply a warm-up." She was genuinely embarrassed, but not to the paralysing extent he had known from his own experience. A faint foreign accent had echoed in her English. He could not quite place it. 'Something Mediterranean,' he thought, 'suits her dark hair as well.'

"I'm sorry, I haven't asked who you are," she suddenly said and walked towards him, stretching her hand.

"Benjamin Faulks," he replied, omitting his title.

"Celeste Leblanc, nice to meet you, *Benjamin*." Her handshake was surprisingly firm for such a thin, graceful build. Her eyes were surprisingly blue for an unusual mocha-coloured complexion. She was more beautiful than any other woman he had ever come across, but it wasn't only her features. Celeste had an enchanting quality about her. She was detached and yet warm, mysterious but soothing.

"Have you got a partner for tonight?" he asked as people started filling the hall, chattering happily.

"Yes, he is supposed to come along," she said and turned to look at the door.

"All right then." He resumed his comfortably-detached manner. 'I might as well watch her dancing,' he thought, 'that is enough of grace for one evening.'

Then the instructor arrived, a short and energetic young man who seemed to have a good eye as to his students' characters. In the course of that evening, they all learned the basic steps of Salsa, a spin or two, what to do with their hands whilst dancing and how to keep their shoulders straight. Benjamin was grateful that the room did not have a mirror, feeling more awkward than ever. But enhanced as his awkwardness was, it did not seem to bother anyone. They were all awkward in one way or another, he thought with surprise, but none of them fussed about it. He envied his younger fellow-dancers for their physical recklessness, for their minimal self-consciousness, for their genuine *joie de vivre*. 'They all enjoy themselves, my dear Faulks,' observed Calista. '*Ela*. You used to know how to do that'.

Step by step, then, Benjamin learned to dance. The first few lessons were slow, tiring, at times insurmountable. His only joy then was to watch Celeste dancing, alone, or with her tall partner. He never ceased to marvel at her glide, so natural, so perfectly in tune with the music. She looked at him every now and then with the compassion of a woman of better fate. They rarely talked, but he felt they bonded in a non-verbal way which was alien to him so far. His days, it seemed, became easier to bear. He waited with growing impatience for Wednesday evenings, and cycled to St. Hugh's regardless of the weather. Celeste was always there, greeting him warmly. Sometimes, he would stop over at the Mitre for a pint on the way home. As the days grew longer, he began to recognise his fellow-dancers on the street, and they would often greet him back with a smile. He had danced with most of them by then, accommodating himself to each woman's rhythm. This new, sensual way of communication had suited him. He felt more at ease, and even his words, which never seemed to fail him, became more fluent.

"An unfamiliar sense of freedom, that's what it is," he told Dr. Wordsworth one afternoon, as they were sitting outside The Bear.

"Salsa, you mean."

"Yes."

"What about Tango, mate? Have you done the Tango as well?"

Benjamin was afraid of Tango. They had a go or two in class, but he never volunteered to try. Watching Celeste succumbing herself to her partner's firm hold was delightful, but he was convinced he could never hold her the same way. On the contrary, he smiled defeatedly to himself, she would have to hold me. It was evident that Celeste felt mostly at home in Tango. 'Must be her warm-blooded Mediterranean spirit,' he thought. From their non-committal conversation he learned that she was half French, half Greek (*Milas Ellenika…?* she asked with delighted surprise as he had told her his wife was Greek), and was writing a DPhil in Classical Archaeology. Nothing more. For the first time in ages, he cursed the Oxford etiquette, wishing he could stuff it and ask her more about herself. The ordinary academic mantra was not enough.

"Tango? Yes, we will start before long," he replied with mock indifference.

"Good," said the doctor, and finished off his pint.

Walking down the cobbled Merton street, Benjamin suddenly noticed that his stride had changed. 'Gosh, I am lighter,' he thought, and for a moment was swept by the glee of a thinning teenager. 'It must be the Guinness,' he smiled to himself, refusing to believe a real change. But the swiftness of his pace stayed. On Wednesday, he decided he would walk up to St. Hugh's instead of cycling. The air was cool and damp, curling around his head. Tango. Tonight it is tango, he thought. Tango with Celeste.

Benjamin knew perfectly well he was not in love with Celeste. 'This cannot be,' he told himself many a time during long hours of rational meditation. He was lucky enough to have lived through love in all its phases, from the fiery swell of passion, through the pain of commitment and into the serenity of mature partnership. The effect Celeste had on him was not recognisable. She was almost unreal in her enchanting beauty, her distant kindness, her silent nature. He was curious, yes, anyone would be, but it was nearly enough just to watch her, or to feel her presence around. 'I am not in love with her, *kallisti mou*. What is it, then? What shall I do?'

'Dance with her', said Calista.

There weren't many people in class that evening, but the numbers were even. "Pretty good for tango," said the instructor, "go grab a partner." Benjamin was slow to react. He was looking around for Celeste, who had escaped his eyes for a moment.

"May I dance with you tonight, Benjamin?" Her soft voice caressed his neck and shoulders.

"It'll be a pleasure."

Holding Celeste felt like holding warm air. Her lightness made her almost invisible, but the mass of soft warmth nestled comfortably in his insecure arms. She shut her eyes obediently as the instructor had said, and waited patiently for him to lead her around the room. Benjamin marvelled at her serene face. She seemed to feel so good anywhere, in every possible situation. He took a deep breath and started walking. There was no music yet, he was free to do as he pleased. He preferred to start with just walking, up and down the hall, turning around every now and then as he came across other couples walking in silence. Some girls were frowning, some nearly stumbled upon their partners' feet. But Celeste was calm, smiling to herself, following him without doubt or judgement.

"How can you feel so secure in a stranger's arms?" he asked as the girls were blinking again.

"I learned to trust them," replied Celeste.

"Was it difficult?"

"Not so much… the harder part was to learn to trust myself," she said and resumed her formal tango posture.

Next they exercised the basic steps. Still no music, but the shuffling of shoes on the wooden floor. Her hold was firmer now, he could feel her weight shifting as she swivelled. She was leaning on him very lightly, as if she chose not to let her mass drop on him for fear of his collapse.

"Do not let me lead you," she whispered.

"Yes, I am doing that, I'm sorry, you're so much better than I am."

"Learn to trust yourself."

"Quite a hard thing to do, you know…"

"Oh, I know," she smiled. "Now lead me."

But Celeste, intuitive and welcoming as she was, was not easily-led. Her skill baffled Benjamin, who stumbled time and again over his own feet. 'This doesn't work,' he kept thinking, his disappointment and despair growing by the second, 'I cannot lead her.' He felt he could no longer adapt to her elegant stride, or hear the steady rhythm of her body. He could not even notice her clear gaze as she examined his face, looking for the sore spot that will explain why her lean had suddenly become a burden.

The class was over. Benjamin thanked Celeste faintly and left as quickly as he could. The way home seemed longer and more tiring than ever.

The next morning, as he flicked through his pigeon-post, he found a small envelope tucked in-between an essay and a couple of notices from the Faculty Offices. Curious, but not letting his curiosity go too far, he assumed this was something from Dr. Wordsworth's clinic, or a college dinner invitation. His name, bar the title, was neatly written in a fountain-pen.

'*Agapitos Benjamin,*' it said, and he smiled at the impossible combination.

'*I am sorry if you found yesterday's class disappointing. I noticed you were distraught, but could not draw your attention and ease your mind.*'

Benjamin's heart leaped with delighted surprise. He did not expect Celeste to approach him, let alone to notice his agony or to care about it.

'*However, I myself was somewhat troubled at the sight of a partner's distress. Tango is all about reciprocity, not to say dependence. I am not free to dance when my partner is distressed, because I take after him.*'

'So this is all about *her dancing,*' thought Benjamin with bitter puzzlement. Nevertheless, not any dancer would go to the trouble of writing a letter to the occasional amateur partner. He continued to read.

'*For some reason, Benjamin, I felt more constrained than I should have when we danced. I do not know why, but I would like to find out. Will you dance with me again? Tonight? Shall we meet outside St. Hugh's at eight?*'

Never in his life had a woman asked to dance with him twice. Not even Calista, whose bold Mediterranean spirit would timidly give in to one or two old-fashioned Greek conventions. There was no question, he will dance with Celeste again.

At eight o'clock, he stood outside St. Hugh's, his hands fidgeting in his pockets. 'Calm down, Faulks, you have been there before,' said Calista with a smile half-amused, half-weary. She was right, in a way. On the other hand though, Calista could not have understood the schoolboy-ish excitement that swirled in his veins. The prettiest woman in class has asked him to dance with her, second time!

"*Kalispera, Benjamin.*" He could not decide in which Celeste felt more at home, Greek or French.

"*Gia sou.*" His Greek accent was fading.

"I see you received my letter," she said.

"I did indeed."

"Good. Listen, I hope you did not think it was too bold... You see, after I had written it I thought, maybe this is too much, maybe you do not understand the ways a dancer's mind works, maybe..."

"Oh, no, it is fine," he replied, averting the chance to disclose his confusion, his English discomfort with up-front women. "Really. I confess I am not a dancer, but I think I understand what you meant."

Celeste shivered involuntarily.

"It's chilly out here, Celeste, why don't we get in?" She smiled with the sweet honesty of a child being caught.

"*On y va?*"

"*On y va.*"

The hall was dark, and unheated. Benjamin fussed with the heaters for a while, watching Celeste shed her scarf, and coat, and *pull-over*, then toss her heavy boots and replace them with those fantastic shoes.

"Ready, Ben?" Ben. Oh, what the hell, he thought, let it be Ben.

"May I call you Ben? you see, it is easier to pronounce."

"Please do." She did not ask whether anyone else had called him that way. He did not tell her that only Wordsworth did, and that they were the only people for whom it had occurred to be natural to do so.

Celeste's shoes were ticking lightly on the wooden floor. She walked towards him, took his hand and led him to the centre of the hall.

"I will reverse the roles now, I'll be the man, you — the woman. This is so that you will learn how to follow. Once you let go, you will also learn the strength of the leader."

She was confident enough. He, as expected but never uttered, had to make a considerable effort to learn the reverse steps. Nevertheless, after a while, Benjamin noticed the ease with which he glided over the floor, held in Celeste's arms. He closed his eyes, letting the scrappy sounds of old Argentinean tangos carry him away. He felt released — what from exactly, he did not care to discover — and his body regained an unfamiliar softness, a blissful ease of movement he did not want to let go of.

Then she stopped. They stood in posture for another moment.

"Thank you, Celeste," said Benjamin as he watched the tiny drops of sweat roll down her temples. "Was it OK?"

"Yes, it was OK," she smiled, to his relief. "I think you understand the *following* now. Shall we try leading?"

"Ah, well, I'm not entirely sure this will work, but I'm willing to try."

"*Loipon.*"

Celeste's hand leaned softly on his arm. She held her arms up, but did not use force to do so. Her back was slightly arched, her head tilted to the left. She held him, but he could hardly feel her grip. 'Almost as if every part of her body has a mind of its own, and they all live in harmony,' he thought, as his limbs felt clumsier than ever.

She was silent and patient. As the first notes of Gardel's *El Dia Que Me Quieras* seeped through the air, she caught Benjamin's eye and with an almost invisible nod made him start. One step back, one to the left, two steps forward. Pause. She glided airily, her legs criss-crossing and brushing through his own. As the music streamed along, Benjamin learned how to read Celeste's movements in the making. Awkwardly, but then generously, he twisted her shoulders so that she could sway. His legs, which nearly stumbled upon her swift criss-crossing, would now form their own criss-crossing, in tandem with hers. He would not shut his eyes as Celeste did, but rather look ahead, afar, until the prudent portraits which circled the hall would dissolve into a grey-brown blur. An involuntary smile, like those of people who had discovered the secret of resolute happiness, was born on his lips. Looking at the heavenly dancer gracefully sharing her gift with him, Benjamin wondered whether she was as exhilarated as he. He could not tell, for her expressions were never disclosing anything more than serenity. 'Does one feel happy while walking, while sleeping?' he asked himself. 'Does one feel happy just living one's life?'

Celeste was immersed in the rhythm, turning obediently as he led her, never for a moment doubting his role. She relied on him, sad, awkward and introverted as he was. He was grateful for that. He was grateful for her silence, for her grace, for the overwhelming sense of freedom that this rigid dance had taught him. When the music stopped, they exchanged no words. Celeste reached out and wiped Benjamin's forehead with a compassionate, passionate gesture. Benjamin's sweat blended with some tears as he offered her a drink of water.

"*Poli orea*, Faulkes," he heard her say.

Ben took Celeste's hands in his and pressed them heartily to his lips. Panting, flush-faced, he was swept over by a warm swell of affection, of comfort, of relief. In fact, he was nearly happy.

Tamar Landau

Blood Lilies

Nearing death, Suella grows patriotic. She puts on yellow rubber gardening gloves and plants an American flag out in the new bed of mulch beside the walk. The flag is generously sized, not as enormous as the one that flies over the Burger King downtown, but big enough for a school or city hall. Its pole is not a flagpole. It is an old tent pole from the back of Mike's pickup truck. He said she could have it when she asked, which was after she had already put the flag up. Mike offered to go out and buy her a real flagpole, one that was longer, so the flag wouldn't droop almost to the ground. His father had been in the service, he told her, and he used to say that if a flag touched the ground, it had to be burnt. Or was it buried? He couldn't remember. Suella was not interested in the way flags died, but she asked which service Mike's father had served in.

Mike climbs in his truck and asks again what cut of beef it is that Suella wants for Sunday dinner. Suella, endearingly cranky, tells him to quit his hollering and just get whatever is on special. Mike says goodnight and makes a slow turnaround. He drives gently because the back of his truck is full of flats of flowers. The dirt driveway is long and heavily rutted, from the old days, when the overseer drove a tractor back and forth between the fields and the house. They called him an overseer, even though the labour was paid, because that was what they had done back home, and anyway, it went with the facade of the house.

Suella does not say goodnight to Mike. She is concentrating on her flagpole. Suella is a hard woman, but harder than usual, lately. Charleen knows why, but she wishes she would be a little nicer, at least to Mike. Suella packs the mulch down around the base of the pole, then backs up to see if it is straight. She does this again and again. The pole looks straight to Charleen, and it doesn't seem very important, anyway, considering there is the big wedding to take care of before the weekend. But usually Suella is all business, especially about weddings and funerals, and Charleen can get the flowers finished all alone, if need be, so she is glad to see Suella doing something that isn't important at this moment.

Charleen is watching Suella work through the plain linen curtains in the kitchen. Suella made the curtains with the finest linen she could find. If you found a good linen, she said, it would outlive you. Charleen has been meaning to embroider the edges. They are a team: Suella sews, Charleen embroiders. She likes that cute little rose pattern from the most recent *Southern Living*. Suella never reads her *Southern Living*, but she won't cancel her subscription and she always pays the bill without complaint. Charleen reads them late at night. She hates to see things go to waste. The subscription is actually Suella's mother's. She has been dead for thirty-two years.

Suella finished the curtains two weeks ago during the long power outage after the first storm of the summer. Three River is all alone on a long dirt road, so it took the electric company almost three days to fix their wires. Suella said she had half a mind to go out there and fix them herself, but Charleen loved it. It was just like in *Gone With The Wind*: she glided around the house with one of the old silver candelabras that sat on a dressing table in one of the guest rooms. Usually, she and Suella sit together in the parlour after supper and read and drink tea, but that night, after she lit Suella's candle, she left the room with a small curtsy. She wanted to change into a gown, but she was embarrassed to do it with Suella awake, even though they had lived together for eight years, nine, in September.

At ten o'clock precisely, Suella found Charleen in the front hall — never used and threaded through with cobwebs — and bent to kiss both of her cheeks, saying, "Good night, Scarlett," and climbing the stairs without so much as a giggle. Charleen wishes her name were Scarlett, or anything but Charleen, but Charleen was her mother's name, so she never tells anyone this. Charleen ran upstairs on tiptoes — which seemed like the only ladylike way to run — unzipped the brittle plastic garment bag in her closet and climbed into her bridesmaid dress from her sister's wedding, tea-length layers of mist-blue tulle. It wasn't quite right, but she didn't want to go through all the old clothes of Suella's great aunts and grandmothers in the guest room closets. That always spooked her.

Anyway, she hardly ever got to wear the blue tulle, after she and her sister had spent night hours planning their weddings, huddled together in the lower bunk, and day hours drawing the dresses with the four-colour pens that Dad got free from the bank. When Sadie had gotten engaged — for real — she and Sadie had gone shopping for dresses, but they hadn't been able to find any nearly as beautiful as the memory, so they had them made, drawing dreams for the seamstress. For a while, when she was in her twenties and even in her thirties, her mother would dutifully remind her, every birthday and Christmas, of the drawing-tablet fashion gallery. "I wish we could have a chance to make the dresses you drew as a child," she would write inside cards, in her tall, old-lady cursive. When Charleen turned forty, her mother — dying — had cut the sketches to fit the slots in the wedding photo album and put them behind the sienna-toned photos of Sadie and Ralph.

The bride loves ivy and wants cascades of it spilling

out from the bouquets, but Suella cannot bring herself to cut it just yet. She tends the vinca, untangling it and curling it around the wires, humming while she works. She is careful not to touch the peonies, as difficult as they are beautiful with their blooms fragile and heavy like onions. She leaves them to Charleen. Charleen is a marvel with flowers. She worked at the greenhouse before she came out to Three River. A couple of greenhouses, actually, both Westwind, next to the Mobil station, and the one out by the Methodist church. Charleen had trouble keeping a job, but not because she isn't good with flowers. She isn't good with people. Or she is too good with them, loves them too much, as she likes to say. At the greenhouses, she always asked to hold customers' babies at the checkout, and sometimes she would have a bit of trouble giving them back, which made people nervous.

Suella loves this about Charleen: she isn't afraid to lay her claim on the world — and it is the whole world, really — and yet she is entirely without selfishness. Charleen has just suggested that they change the name of the farm to Sleeping Beauty Farm. Suella herself has often considered changing the name to Old Maid Farm, in defiance and possession. But Sleeping Beauty Farm is no more arbitrary, she supposes.

When Charleen had first come to Three River, she asked where the rivers were. Suella said there were none, as far as she knew — she had not thought of this since she was a child. The next morning, Charleen left a note on the breakfast table, saying, 'In search of the three,' dramatically underscored. Suella wondered where she had found the purple crayon. Charleen hadn't come home until after dark, bug-bitten and brown with sun and dirt. She hadn't found anything except a few puddles, and she was upset, almost offended, it seemed to Suella. Suella told her that the only thing she knew was that the farm had been called Three River for almost a hundred and fifty years. Then she added, "I guess it's a mystery."

"A mystery," Charleen had nodded eagerly, very satisfied with this, as though naming not-knowing changed it from frightening to romantic. A couple of weeks later, Charleen had read an article on global warming in a *Newsweek* at the dentist's office. "That accounts for the rivers drying up!" she exclaimed, all her suspicions about the value of reading *Newsweek* confirmed. Suella bought her a subscription of her own for her birthday.

Suella had not suggested then that perhaps there had never been any rivers, that perhaps Three River had just seemed apt, but yesterday she said that Sleeping Beauty did not seem a very apt name for a farm. Charleen said, "But it's such a beautiful story. I love the part about how she sleeps for a hundred years and wakes up just as young and beautiful as she ever was for her prince." Suella had not ever been beautiful, but Charleen had been. She had seen pictures: Charleen at her sister's wedding, in the blue tulle gown she still kept in her closet and tried on sometimes when she thought Suella was asleep, Charleen young in a sundress that tied on the shoulders, Charleen in a hat — borrowed, Charleen had said indignantly: her family didn't have that kind of money! — like a beekeeper's, with a net that came down over her eyes. Anyway, looking at Charleen, Suella could not help but say yes, so she asked Mike to bring the sign when he came up from the market today. She noticed it missing last week when Mike took her to her doctor's appointment. He said it had fallen down a while ago and he had it in his shed back at home. Mike says 'home' rarely and haltingly, but Suella pretends not to notice, because nobody likes a meddler. If Mike wants to tell her about his wife, he will.

Suella tries to remember what the sign looks like. She has not seen it in years; she can't remember the last time she left the farm before her doctor's appointments. These days, she gets only as far as the cherry blossoms halfway down the drive, and that far only once or twice a spring, when Charleen can pull her down, threatening that they will fall any day, that they have already started to shrivel. Suella loves the brambles of white, too, and the way they hang close around that dark, damp drive. They used to call it Ralston Lane, she tells Charleen every spring, back when Daddy Ralston was alive. Every spring Charleen and Suella argue a bit about whether the pink or the white is more beautiful, but Charleen isn't much of a debater, particularly not under the cherry trees, where she twirls and twirls, swimming in their sweet, heavy scent, protesting giddily that cherry trees shouldn't grow in the northeast, and especially not here in the shade.

When Charleen first came, they walked down the driveway together early every morning, pulling two old Radio Flyers full of flowers in jars marked '50 c,' '75 c' and '$1.00.' They had a stand out by the road, a pretend covered-wagon with a Tupperware container to hold the money. Charleen made the 0's of the '$1.00' sign into the eyeballs of a face, and she cried the morning they found shrivelled irises and snapdragons strewn on the ground, like the remains of a wedding procession or a cortege. Suella said the money was no big deal. Charleen wasn't even thinking about money. She wished that they had taken the flowers, too. "Just to leave them here, to die? It's beastly!" she said. That was the end of the Three River flower stand. Later, Charleen learned "barbaric" from *Newsweek*'s coverage of Sadaam Hussein, and she used that word when she repeated the story at dinner.

Mike's pickup is crawling up the driveway now.

Suella can see the dust rising. He is right on schedule: it is 7.15. Charleen comes out. She sleeps later than Suella, usually, but she is always out to greet Mike. She says good morning to Suella and stands beside her, waving vigorously to Mike. When she sees he has groceries, she runs to help him unload the car, even when he tells her there are only two bags. Humming, Charleen takes the groceries inside, the screen door clapping shut behind her. Looking at his thighs, arms crooked at the elbow, Mike brings the sign over to Suella. He lays it face down on the ground.

"Let's see," says Suella.

Mike doesn't move. She turns it over. 'Three River Farm' has been scratched out, and in the wood is crudely inscribed, 'Old Dyke Farm.'

Suella looks up at him silently. He looks at it as if for the first time, squinting.

"How long has it been like this?" she asks.

"I don't know."

Mike, of course, took the sign down long ago, and she knows this. He wouldn't have mentioned it at all if she hadn't noticed it missing. She understands now why he kept making excuses when she asked him about it, as though if he waited another couple of days, it would be a moot point. Ever since she told him about the cancer, he has expected her to drop dead any second. Still, he never wants to talk about it. Men are embarrassed to use the word 'breast,' thinks Suella, although she catches him looking sideways at her droopy profile, as though he might catch a glimpse of a great, consuming lump.

"How long, Mike?" She is firm, but gentle: he hates to see them hurt.

"A few years."

"Since when?"

"Oh, a little while after the thugs wrecked the stand."

Charleen is approaching, and Mike moves to turn the sign over, but Suella holds his arm.

"Oh, you brought it up!" She exclaims as she walks up. "Suella, I told you, we don't have to change the sign. It doesn't need to be official. I just thought you and I and Mike could call it 'Sleeping Beauty,' just between us... Oh, what's this? Old Dyke Farm! So is that where the rivers went!"

Suella can't tell if this is a question or an exclamation. Either way, she does not say anything, just watches Charleen.

"Someone must know their history around here, huh? I didn't know there was a dike at all. None of the books at the library said anything about it. But I guess there must be three of them, somewhere upriver, huh? That's a perfect name. Even better than Sleeping Beauty Farm."

Suella thinks of saying that the anonymous benefactor could have at least consulted them, but sarcasm would crush Charleen. There is no time to speak before Charleen rushes on, anyway. "Remember that story about Peter with his thumb in the dike? He saved all of Norway! Or was it Sweden?"

Mike turns away and looks at the long, green fields, lying fallow. They have not been planted since Suella's mother died. Suella looks at Charleen, long and hard. "It was Holland, I think."

"What's the difference between a dike and a dam, anyhow?" Suella shrugs, but Charleen is excited and will not be deterred. "I wonder what they were trying to save!" Charleen says. "Must have been our little farm here!"

"Must have been," says Suella.

Later, when Charleen is in the kitchen, cutting the sandwiches into little shapes with a set of cookie cutters she ordered off the home-shopping network, Suella tells Mike not to put the sign up again. Mike is glad to acquiesce. He does not like conflict, especially with anonymous vandals, unseen enemies. His wife used to say that all enemies were unseen. She said that often, and dramatically, when she called after he moved out — after eleven years — resigned his position at City Hall, and took the job at Ernie's Market.

He did this for reasons he couldn't explain. He didn't even try to explain when — three years later — she came to the Market, shaking her head and sputtering. She had heard he was living with two women. "Is that what you wanted, Michael? Is that what you were looking for?" He did not tell her that they were two old women who never left their thirty-one acres, or that he wasn't even living with them, that he had never been inside the great decrepit mansion that belonged more in Mississippi than in New England, that he just brought them groceries and prescriptions on his way to work and stocked the old metal bookcase outside Ernie's with their flowers. It did not occur to him then. He just repeated an apology that didn't sound very sincere — although he was fairly certain it was — until she shook her head and told him he was living in a fantasy world, that he had somehow had managed to un-grow up, that he didn't know what he wanted and probably never would. Mike loved her for her understanding of people.

He lives with those two sinful women now. When Suella found out about her cancer, she said she would feel better if there were someone who could drive at the farm. He didn't much like living alone, anyway, so Suella moved him into one of the guest rooms on the first floor. The green velvet drapes keep out the sun during the day, so he can sleep; there are French doors that lead out onto the patio, where the three of them eat a late lunch together, but he never uses them. He goes out the main entrance and walks around the house to meet Charleen and Suella for tuna sandwiches, carrot sticks, and lemonade. This is Charleen's favourite lunch. Charleen calls tuna 'tunafish salad,' and calls the sandwiches she makes with it 'Howdy Doodies.' She makes them on pumpernickel bread that she bakes herself, from scratch. Suella has learned to like tuna on pumpernickel. She asked Mike if Charleen's name for them was a New England convention. Mike said he thought it was Charleen's convention. Charleen, overhearing — that woman did have good ears — said everybody knew that you got to name the things that you invented.

Charleen is sharp, thinks Mike, sharper than either he or Suella usually gives her credit for being. She found the report from Suella's doctor folded in the second-to-lowest drawer of an old velvet-lined jewellery box in one of the guest rooms. Then, to figure out what it meant, she read all the Health/Medicine sections of her old *Newsweeks*, which she kept in chronological order in cardboard boxes in her closet. When she asked Mike about when Suella would start the chemotherapy — she hid a guilty smile at the word — she said that she knew Suella wouldn't tell her a thing about it, so she wasn't going to waste her breath asking. Her precious breath, she said. She wasn't going to waste her precious breath, so Mike might as well just forget all this closed-mouthed business. Mike isn't sure whether he should have told her about it, but Charleen seemed fearless, then, cutting the tuna fish salad sandwiches diagonally, decisively, down the middle.

Charleen is in the kitchen mixing up some of her secret recipe flower juice for the tiger lilies, which Suella says look wan. Charleen told Suella her secret recipe, even the part about the pinch of garlic, which — as Mike has pointed out — made it not very secret at all. Anyway, Suella insists that Charleen makes it better. It is magic, thinks Charleen. She is glad to be magic. If she had not told her secret, she thinks, she would never have known that she was magic. She does not much like keeping secrets, anyway, even little secrets, like the flower juice recipe. She has a big secret now: it is that Suella's secret is not a secret. Charleen giggles out loud.

Suella is outside, working on her flag again. She has been humming a lot, lately. Even singing, sometimes. Suella sings well, and she knows all the old songs; when Charleen is singing and making up words, Suella asks if she wants to know what the real words are. Sometimes Charleen says no, and that doesn't bother Suella a bit, but usually she says yes and repeats the lyrics after Suella until she remembers them. Anyway, Charleen is glad that Suella is singing. She is too quiet most of the time. Charleen pours some flower juice into a tumbler and takes it and the watering can outside.

"Do you think the flagpole needs something on top?" Suella asks when Charleen comes out.

"On top?"

"You know, like the flagpoles in the parades on TV. What is that, that they put on top?"

"I don't know. Maybe Uncle Sam?"

Suella starts laughing way back in her throat. She drops her shovel and stands there, laughing, with her yellow gloves away from her sides just a little bit. Charleen starts laughing, too, even though she was not kidding.

"Oh, Charleen, you are a riot, girl." Suella calls Charleen 'girl,' sometimes. Charleen thought it was strange, at first, but she is, after all, six years, two months, and thirteen days younger than Suella. "Well, I don't know either, but I think it looks kind of naked. We'll have to think on that."

"I brought you the flower juice," says Charleen.

"Thank you, ma'am. Would you put it on those tigers for me?"

Charleen does not know why Suella is so concerned about the tiger lilies, which look fine and are not included in any of the bouquets for the wedding, but she does not argue. "I brought some flower juice for you, too."

"For me?"

"You're looking mighty pale yourself."

Suella looks her up and down, real slow, like they used to in the Wild West movies before a gunfight. "Oh, Charleen, I'm just fine. Just as healthy as I've ever been."

"Well, it's for you," Charleen says, awkwardly twisting the tumbler into the mulch bed where Suella is working. She turns to the tiger lilies, wishing that Suella had not lied, that Suella would just tell her so she wouldn't have to think of a way to pretend-discover it. It is a different kind of secret, now, one that Suella covered up, not just one that Suella kept to herself. Charleen read an article in *Newsweek* about husbands' attitudes toward breast cancer. The wife was supposed to anticipate him acting like she had been raped, penetrated by something shapeless, dark, malevolent. Charleen read the article twice before she understood that the woman was supposed to expect her husband to fault her, to find her weak, beaten, corrupted.

Mike watches Father Dowling every night on the little TV in his room — Suella and Charleen do not have a television — just before he goes to work. Once upon a time, leaving the silent farm, he often imagined that he was making a getaway from some crime too mysterious to know, to terrible to remember. After he turned around in two slow, smooth arcs, he used to indulge himself and drive to the end of the driveway with his headlights off.

It seems a little silly now to do this now, because he is always careful to look under his pickup before he starts it. Back when Suella was alone on the farm, with him bringing her groceries and mail once a week, a stray cat had found its way out to Three River, and Mike had driven away with it still under the truck. Suella had considered the cat some kind of providence: farms needed cats, she said, and Three River was no exception. When that lonesome cat swelled with kittens, he thought it was a miracle, but Suella said nobody ever heard of a farm with just one cat; when the kittens were born, Suella said she figured they'd have to name them. Women, he protested, were better at names, then — uncannily open — he confided that his wife used to talk about what they would name their children. Suella put her hand over his mouth gently — it was the first time she had touched him, and he was shocked by the coarseness of her skin — and said, "All you have to do, mister, is listen." She touched each kitten lightly above its eyes and whispered its name to him — or maybe to the kitten, he couldn't tell. He didn't remember anymore what she had named the kittens, but when she got to that great grey cat, its flaccid belly still heaving with the exhaustion of childbirth, she said simply, "Mother."

She called him that night at work. Mother had been sleeping under his pick-up truck when he pulled out, she said. She was dead. He apologised profusely and asked her if she was all right. She said that she didn't call for sympathy. Sympathy was cheap, she said coldly, and asked him to bring her baby formula on the way home from work. He brought it to her and then stopped by again, two days later. She did not come to the window, so he blazed into the house, making himself brave, ready to hoist her over his shoulder and rescue her. She was not there. He found her in the barn, in a corner streaming with lines of morning-white light. She was pressing a tiny ball of fur to her breast, exposed pale. "Drink, drink," she was urging the kitten, begging it, "Please, drink." Mike still wonders if she could possibly have expected those ancient, parched, childless breasts to swell with milk.

When she came out, she was holding the kitten. She told him that she had already buried the other kittens, two yesterday and one the day before. He looked at her and then at the kitten in her arms, trying to discern whether it was still alive. He offered to call the veterinarian, but she was already turning stiffly toward the house, cradling the kitten in two hands like a piece of pottery she had unearthed, a fragile vestige of another world.

It is almost eight a.m., which is late even for Charleen, so Suella goes in to check on her. She worries, sometimes, about Charleen's health, because if Charleen gets going on a project, she forgets to eat, and she is diabetic — just a smidge, Charleen always protests. Suella hears the music is playing on Charleen's radio, Granddaddy's old one with a lifetime warranty from Sears-Roebuck (how confused the repairman had been, last month, when he saw the light-up radium dial and the imposing knobs). Her grandfather had built his fortune on wise investments like that warranty, her father had always said, but Suella knows, watching the shingles slide, feeling the columns sag, that the beginning of all of it, an old-style plantation in New Hampshire, had not been wise.

The music is crackly country-western from some station in Boston. Charleen is singing along tunelessly, cutting jaggedly in time to the music. Suella knocks and then opens the door at the same time Charleen says, "Come in."

Charleen is sprawled on her great four-poster bed, propped up on her elbows, dismembering the Georgia O'Keefe calendar Suella gave her for Christmas. A few prints are already stuck haphazardly to the faded gold velveteen wallpaper. "I decided I liked the pictures better when I couldn't see the days," Charleen says shortly.

"What about your poems?"

"Poems?"

Every night before bed, Charleen fills the box of the day with an observation, five or six words, a prepositional phrase, a metaphor: 'deer across the field, fleeting as thought' or 'impatiens spreading like measles.' She calls it her journal, but Suella — who records the meals and events of every day in a small leather book as carefully as if she were balancing a chequebook, preparing for a reckoning — calls it poetry. Charleen always lets Suella read her calendars. Suella cannot bring herself to share her own journal, though it seems to her infinitely less personal than the day-images of the calendar.

"You know, your journal."

"I decided I didn't want to keep a journal anymore. There's nothing to remember, these days."

"Oh." Suella watches her closely.

Charleen looks up. "I mean... I don't want to remember these days." Charleen's eyes are puddly deep, her gaze — and that is what it is, a gaze — silvery wise. Suella feels something swelling in her chest. She wonders if it could be her tumour.

Charleen and Suella are working on the bouquets for the wedding, now. Suella has just risen from the wicker divan on the patio, where she lay after lunch, her arms straight by her sides, as though she could not bear to relax. Charleen cut the flowers alone, thinking about how ill Suella must be to refuse fresh lemonade.

They work on the dining room table on a great wooden table that seems to Charleen to belong in a castle. Charleen makes the first of each different arrangement — for the bridesmaids and the altar and the chancel — and Suella copies. She always asks a lot of questions, so Charleen thinks it might be faster if she just made everything, but she doesn't tell Suella this. They always work on the bride's bouquet together.

Charleen wishes that Suella would quit her singing, now. She has gotten stuck on two songs, *Round her Neck* and *Tie a Yellow Ribbon*. They are both about servicemen coming home to their girls. Suella had a serviceman away in the Second War. He hadn't died. He had just decided that he didn't want her anymore. Charleen knows about him because she found some of the old letters in that same guest room where Suella keeps all her secrets. But Suella knows that the serviceman secret isn't a secret any more, because Charleen asked her about him.

Suella wasn't mad about her snooping. She just said that there wasn't much to tell. Then she talked for an hour. Suella had worn a yellow ribbon 'round her neck, just like the song said, she told Charleen, and John had never come home to untie it for her. Maybe it was just as well, Charleen thought, remembering the scary story in Suella's collection of children's books where a woman untied the ribbon around her neck on her wedding night — or had her husband untied it? — and her head fell off. Suella's father, Daddy Ralston, thought it was just as well, too, because he hadn't thought very highly of John, Suella told Charleen. Daddy Ralston said Suella lost all her ambition when she met John; she lost interest in the Catullus and Virgil he had taught her to love. When John came along, all that schooling of hers just flew out of her mind, he had said, and all she wanted to read was books for her class, children's books — she was teaching first-grade at the elementary school. It turned out, though, that after John, she stopped reading at all. That next year, she quit her job and spent her time at Three River, cooking and sewing. When she told the story to Charleen, she called it coming back home. Charleen does not understand how she ever really left.

Charleen looks out the window nervously, as though the angel she has put on top of the flagpole might have flown away. Earlier, she passed by the closet where they keep the Christmas decorations and thought of the porcelain-faced angel, delicate and virginal and all in white. She found it and took it outside with her. She hopes that Suella is pleased. Suella keeps looking at the flag, but she hasn't said anything about the angel yet. She just keeps singing *Tie a Yellow Ribbon 'Round the Old Oak Tree*. Charleen joins her and sings for two or three lines before she realises that it is the wrong thing to do.

Mike has told her that Suella's hair will fall out when she starts chemotherapy next week, that she will be very ill and her hair will fall out. Charleen dreamed about it last night, dreamed herself brushing short tufts of white and watching them come loose between her fingers like cotton from the tree. She dreamed that she wrote in a July box on her calendar, 'Hair harvested, fields fallow.' Charleen keeps touching her own hair, making sure it is still there, silvery-grey and smooth and long. She is glad that she cut time apart this morning, cut it apart and hung it on the walls.

They are sitting down to dinner. Mike spent the afternoon clearing fallen branches from the woods that straddle the driveway, but he knows better than to come to Suella's table in his workclothes, so he is damp from the shower. The women have moved the wedding arrangements out to the patio for his compliments, but they do not say anything about them. He looks at them while Suella gets the potatoes from the oven and Charleen sprinkles the salad with Parmesan cheese. She sprinkles everything with Parmesan cheese.

Mike says, "They look beautiful, ladies." He knows only what he has gleaned from Charleen about growing flowers, and nothing about arranging them. "Are you finished?"

"Just the bride's bouquet left," replies Charleen, sitting down.

Suella says, "You best stop ogling those flowers before they wilt from your eyes. Come over here and eat your dinner while it's hot." She pours iced tea and abruptly walks outside as the ice pops in the tall glasses.

"What is she doing?" Charleen wonders softly. Suella strides to the flag and takes the angel from its top.

"What was that doing up there?" Mike asks.

"I put it up. To cover the top of the pole. I hope she's not angry."

"An angel? Why an angel?" Charleen does not answer. She is watching Suella crown the flagpole with a star that they used to put on the small Christmas tree in the parlour. This is not the question that he really wants to ask, anyway. He wants to know if Suella knows that Charleen knows about the cancer. He doesn't understand why she doesn't want her to know, anyway. Suella and Charleen know all each other's stories; it would be something new to talk about, anyway, and God knows, more important than any of the things they actually do talk about.

Suella smiles and stands next to the star-topped flagpole like she is posing for a photograph. Mike is struck by how distant she looks behind the window screen.

"Why did she hold off until we were all sitting down to dinner?" asks Charleen, serving herself strawberries, fresh from the garden and red all the way through.

She wanted an audience, thinks Mike, but he does

not respond: Suella is opening the door and Charleen is saying, "That's beautiful, Suella. Really, it's perfect. I'm sorry about the angel."

Suella waves her hand in the air. "Oh, forget the angel. You had the right idea, though. I would never have thought of the star if you hadn't put Christmas tree crowns in my head."

Charleen beams. "Well, the star is much better, anyway. Just like the stars on the flag. What does the blue stand for on the flag? Courage, or something, isn't it?"

Mike lets Suella answer. "Loyalty. The blue is for loyalty." There is a pause.

"It should stand for the sky. The blue should. That's what it looks like, out there," Charleen says, beckoning toward the pole. "It looks like you pulled a star out of the sky and put it on top of the pole."

Mike doesn't understand the way Charleen thinks, but he likes it. Suella asks him to pass the peas.

After dinner, Mike does the dishes while the women finish the bridal bouquet. They shut themselves in Suella's bedroom because the patio doesn't have a door and they say it's bad luck for men to see the bouquet before the ceremony. As he is trying to wash the colander, he hears the door open and close, and then Charleen's girlish run down the hall. She is excited, breathless, and asks him if he can spare an hour tonight after Suella goes to bed. She needs to go out, she says, but she's not a very good driver.

She's a terrible driver, Mike thinks, and she doesn't even have a license. "It's a date," he says.

"I'll tell you more on the way," Charleen says. "But until then, not a word to Suella. Not one word."

Mike nods, but she is already running back down the hall. He settles down in the wicker rocker with one of Charleen's *Newsweeks*. The president is on the cover, and he falls asleep almost before he opens it.

Charleen wakes him, clapping her hand over his mouth. She pulls him out to the truck. She is carrying a spade. Mike tries to take it from her to put it in the back, but she holds firm — she is stronger than he imagined — and whispers that it will clank around and wake Suella. She asks him to please start the car quietly. He tries not to laugh and shows her the 'N' on the gearshift.

They are rolling down the driveway, the only sound the gravel underneath the wheels. Charleen asks him why he doesn't turn his lights on. "They don't make any noise, do they?"

He doesn't know whether she is being sarcastic, but he is honest when he says that he doesn't want to ruin the view. The sky is like a blank movie screen, lit mauve by something dim and far behind, and the trees are black against it.

"Like they got cut out of the sky," Charleen says.

"Like they got cut out of the sky," Mike repeats, looking at her.

They are whispering, even though they are far from the house. As they slow almost to a stop, just beyond the cherry blossoms, Mike turns on the engine. Charleen looks to him in alarm. "Don't worry," he says. "We're almost a mile out."

"Almost a mile?"

He nods.

"The cherry blossoms are almost a mile out?" Charleen is incredulous.

"Yeah." He tries to keep the of-course sound out of his voice.

"Just think. All those times we go out to see the cherry blossoms, we walk almost a mile. And then back! So almost two miles."

Mike does not know what to say.

"We're going downtown," says Charleen. "We need

some flowers."

"What do you need?"

"You'll see." She is coy.

"Charleen, it's ten o'clock. The only place that's going to be open is the grocery store. They don't have anything that you haven't got in your backyard."

"Trust me. I know what I'm doing."

And Mike does trust her. As they reach the first traffic light, Mike asks, "Where to?"

"Go to Memorial Park."

"Memorial Park?"

"Yes." And then they are there, at the long, narrow island that separates the westbound traffic from the eastbound traffic on Central Avenue. There is a blinking yellow light on the first lamppost, ever since the night that old, blind Mrs. Daniels beached her Oldsmobile up on the curb. Mike can never remember what he is supposed to remember: war casualties, or the service of all the veterans, dead or alive, or the founding fathers, or all the town's departed citizens. Mike has never understood the difference between all those holidays that people take on Mondays for their convenience, Veterans' Day, Memorial Day, Labor Day. Ernie's Market is open twenty-four hours a day every day except Christmas. Charleen has asked him if that doesn't bother him. It doesn't, actually; as he tells her, he needs that.

Charleen tells him not to stay waiting, to come back for her in twenty minutes, and kisses his cheek. She slips out of the truck as easily as liquid.

The next morning, Mike drives home with Hershey bars for Suella and Charleen, plain for Suella, with almonds for Charleen. He is eager to see what Charleen has done with her loot. She called them blood lilies. She invented the name but she was sure it was the right name, exactly right. There are six of them, purplish stalks almost four-and-a-half feet tall crowned with one huge, yawning scarlet blossom. They were seductive even in the bed of his truck. He had driven away too fast, forgetting that her spade was in the back, so she had dug the flowers out of the ground at Memorial Park lustily, with her hands. The way the flowers were spotlighted next to the great, granite slab of names, she said, made them so dramatic, so beautiful that they were painful. "It shouldn't be that way," said Charleen, with a conviction that she was too old to have. He thought that this was her defence, even though he hadn't said anything about stealing the flowers, but he wasn't sure if this was the reason she had to have them or the reason she could take them.

That same morning, Charleen wakes up early and is not tired at all, although she was up half the night. She can never sleep when she gets excited. She eats breakfast very fast. It is strange to be awake before Suella is up and Mike is home. Three River is very quiet. She diligently avoids the blood lilies, although she planted them in the dark and yearns to see them in the light. There is work to be done. On the patio, the bridal bouquet is already sealed in a white box with a Three River sticker. She packages the other arrangements and stacks the boxes on the driveway for Mike to put in the back of the truck. She works very efficiently. Mike will take the flowers into town as soon as he gets home. The wedding is at noon.

That same morning, when Suella goes to the kitchen for her shredded wheat, an orange juice glass is already in the sink and there are several Honey Nut Cheerios bobbing in some off-colour milk in a bowl on the counter. Honey Nut Cheerios are Charleen's favourite, but she does not drink the milk after she eats the cereal. She says that it is all yucked up. The milk is Suella's favourite part of the cereal. She can feel herself getting stronger when she drinks it. She hears Mike's car in the driveway, and she finishes her cereal and goes outside to help Mike and Charleen with the wedding flowers.

That same morning, they stand, the three of them, knowing and not knowing, looking at — watching — Charleen's blood lilies, arching back in a circle around the flagpole, like they were dancing, like they were dying.

Stephanie Frank

Last Light

Bernard ran his slow finger down the cards. Nannies, rabbits, violin lessons. The dark rain chased his gaze down the frozen window, ran into his palm and soaked his cuff.

Canford Primus (paraffin) £2

The finger stopped. This was exactly what it wanted. Bernard stepped in and read the dusk-blue card. It was a beautifully written spider-sprawl of letters. He strained to read the pattern. No telephone number or address, just some directions and a tiny feather-map. He raised his glasses on his damp nose and saw even wavelets and three-stroke tussocks and a stick-pier. Somewhere on the sea front, and a little out of town, was a primus stove, price £2. He hadn't been that far for years. The wind was too cold and walking too hard, and everywhere to sit was wet. Besides Irene wouldn't leave the house, and the memory of sun and foam and children's toes was not his to bear alone. He would see tomorrow.

Irene was dozing in the faded chair, oblivious to the take-away television sounds that crackled their way along the pipes and muffled themselves with carpet tiles. He tapped her mottled arm lightly with his hat.

I found a stove — it's only £2.

He said, but no sound came out, because Irene was deaf and it made no difference whether he spoke or didn't. She smiled and resealed her eyes and slept again. Bernard went into the other room and sat down on the bed. It was some time before he moved to take off his world-wet clothes, but when he had, he laid them on the floor and made himself some tea.

The toaster curled into his lap warmed his thighs.

Its spring had long ago unwound and a firm hand kept the bread in place like a kitten underwater. The first burnt-bone slice he buttered and handed to Irene. The second, which was worse, he ate himself. Dessert was bread and sweet purple jam and tea. He rinsed the plates and laid them on the floor, and settled Irene deep inside her chair.

Then he sat on the comfortable bed and watched the world. They had two rooms and the brown bathroom, but only one chair, so Bernard spent his time on the bed and watched the weather. Nothing ever happened at 20ft high, but in winter and in summer he waited for something.

Night came behind blue clouds, and he made them both ready for bed. Pushing the plates aside he laid his wife on the sheets and settled her head, and moved a fine-spun hair from her pink mouth. He turned off the light and lay down himself and fell asleep. A few moments later the street lamp by the window thrummed into life and covered Irene in gold.

It was a wet day, and Bernard felt the weight of the long walk ahead drag at his arms as he dressed. It was cold in the flat and he heaped a blanket onto Irene's sleep-filled form. Then he went down the stairs and out into the water daylight.

Sheltered by the winding streets of stunted houses, his shoes began to suck at the pavements. Round the edge of the town he pushed on, smelling the sea and feeling its sticky fingers pressing down his coat and round his ankles. Finally, diving through the last band of expressionless buildings, he came to the seafront. The pale sea came as it had done all his life, surging towards the beach from some far place. Ranging hungrily, its ever-rolling never brought it closer to the land, and Bernard felt a sudden pity for the waves. Away to his left he saw the pier, and crossed the road and the grey-grass dunes to the shingle. The surf kneaded the stones at its edge, moving them up and down the same width of beach. In a thousand years this might be glorious golden sand, but now it was a mire around his feet and soaked his shoes. As he climbed along towards the brown-legged pier, he searched to the left, unsure of what he was looking for. The dunes widened. Birds hid in hollows scooped out by summer children with their hands. He began to wish he was not there. But necessity had driven him too far from home, and he fought forward.

There was a beach hut, tiny and dull green amongst the fading grasses. Its roof was battered tar-paper, and getting closer he saw a flaking railed platform in front of it, and a row of jam jars. He hauled himself upwards, bending his head down against the wind that raked over the dune-top. Curtains were drawn at the window. He wondered who lived here. Squatters perhaps, or youths smelling paint. He stopped and helplessness and fear came round him, but the cold came too and he went on.

Have you come about the stove?
The voice came through the curtained glass.
Yes.

He leant on the rail and it moved towards the sea. The wave-roar was loud in the back of his head, and the wind effortlessly bludgeoned his word back into his throat. The bleach-blue material moved and a shadow studied Bernard's aching body. He didn't hear the bolts lifted back, or see the top half of the door begin to yaw, then the wind threw that against him too and he fell down.

I'm sorry.
A pale figure was beside him and he was rising.

That was the last thing you needed.

And he found himself sitting in a warm darkness and forgot his life.

Went about nine o'clock this morning I'm afraid. I didn't think it would go so fast. I didn't think anyone used them any more.

He needed to see the eyes he knew ran beside the low voice. He put up a hand to remove and wipe his spectacles, but it fell back.

You can't see anything through those can you? Let me dry them.

And they were gone from his face. He tried to thank her, but Bernard had not spoken for a long time, and instead a ball of spittle scratched itself from his throat and fell against his bottom teeth.

She lent forward, warm hands coming behind his ears and suddenly he saw the soft skin of her eyes and white lashes and then they moved back into the dark.

I hope that's better.

He tried to reply, but again he let the wind hiding in his throat snatch back his words. He tried to cough, and choked.

Would you like something to drink? I only have orange squash or there's plain water.

A blur and a clink and a cut-cold glass in his hand.

I'm so sorry I can't help you. You must have come a long way. I'm Anne.

She extended a smile and Bernard felt smooth fingers work their way into his fist. He had not coughed for half an hour, and now slow-mumbled a reply.

Bernard.

Pleased to meet you.

His fist kneaded the near air.

It does get dark early these days, I'll light a lamp.

He watched her move away and bend and pause. A flame rose and began to burn the air. She sat in a rocking chair that brought her close then far without a sound. It lit her face then covered it. The candle-shadow sketched for him the facets of a rare rich jewel that glinted in his mind and threw patterns on his memory.

I'm sorry to have to turn you out, but I must get on. You shouldn't be out in the dark. Not these days.

Bernard nodded and rose, but every joint screamed at him to let them rest a while longer on this bed and in this place.

Thank you.

He couldn't think of anything to add.

My pleasure, you're very welcome to drop in if you're nearby. I don't get many visitors!

She smiled and held the door open onto the black-grey wind.

Good bye.

He stepped into the cold and she was gone.

Now the gusts were now behind him and glided his shoes over the wet-stone beach. Weaving through the wind, his eyes did not see.

He tried to dream and found his imagination rusted under the loam of fifty years. He hardly dared to touch the fine mechanism in case it broke him. But against his past the little flame licked and worked. Time began to move in him once more and started spinning the ever-widening wheels of longing, fervour, power and dread. It span thread too, questions strung behind him on the wind like streamers at a carnival of want and wondrous speculation. There was a fire-teasing in his soul and Bernard fuelled it gladly with a plethora of new-born thoughts. He crossed the sodium-soaked tarmac without a glance and joined the shadows of the town. In the dark, the rain fell all about him and could not seem to touch him.

When he woke up in the morning the rapture was replaced by fear. Fear that he would lose this new-found freedom, fear he would forget these new-found thoughts. He begged his memory to produce some evidence, some scrap or shiver of the change of yesterday. And it revealed a warmth within him, a lightness in his body and an image of two dim walls and an old woman by a candle lamp. So he fell back on the pillow and felt tired by his relief.

Later he helped Irene onto her ghost-feet and led her to the shower. Her sleeping eyes filled with falling water but she was gummed and dreaming, unaware of rain in some far distant land. He dried her gently and made toast and tea and stood and ate, watching her sleep, her peace, drift up and down with the pink plaid rug.

There was still no stove and Bernard's energy could not enfold, warm the dosing Irene in its ardour. He took his hat and coat and went again into the pin-grey town with its damp plastic bags and peeling meters. No one came to this place. Even in the wet, the early Christmas decorations were dusty behind the pitted glass. This was a bitter, acned town, and the wind-driven spume had coated it in winter.

There was nothing in the window, or on the back-buckled cards behind the supermarket checkouts. He bought some biscuits and tea. He wanted to be by the sea. That was all, and the need pushed him out of the town. The diurnal street lamps craned to hear his questions as he hurried through their gold liquid-pyramids. Who was she, and why and how?

He hummed up and down scales with his footfalls, warming up like a singer for a great performance, so he could ask her, agree with her, share anecdotes and past times. He was happy. He had a purpose. He desperately wanted to see the ashen horizon underlining that place that was no longer his past but only his future. And he came onto the scene that stretched forever to either side and went into the lead-leafed dunes.

He knocked and this time stood back, wondering over the neat green front. He saw the drained curtains twitch minutely, and had to close his eyes.

Hullo. I didn't think you'd be back so soon! Come in.

One half of the door, then the other and he was back again. He could see now in the morning what was inside the hut. Along one wall a mattress lying on three boxes, cupboards across the far end, a tiny square table on which he saw the lamp of the previous night, and before that, a rocking chair.

She opened her palm towards the bed, and sat herself on the edge of the chair.

Do you often walk along the beach? I've never seen you.

I haven't for a long time. I'd forgotten how pleasant it was. BERNARD LET HIMSELF GO.

Yes, I never tire of looking at the sea.

HE NEEDED TO KNOW. How, how long have you lived here?

Almost twelve years now. Then immediately, Have you found another stove?

Bernard shook his head. One of the questions.

HE WANTED TO HELP. You should have asked more than £2 for it. They can go for ten secondhand.

Oh, I only needed £2.

She smothered the question with an answer and Bernard leaned eagerly into her words.

I wanted to buy Mr. X some gloves for Christmas, I saw some lovely thermal ones for £9.99, and I've already got the rest.

He needed time to think. He wanted to tell someone.

I must go. A power he did not notice hauled him to his feet.

Won't you stay for a drink?

Sorry, I have to go.

Well, maybe you'll drop by another day.

Yes, thank you, good bye.

Back on the road, he leant hard on a lamp-post. Excitement and fear fought around him. He knew he had to get back to the flat before his mind consumed his body and left him no way to walk.

He found Irene asleep on the toilet with her rug over her knees and suddenly saw iniquity slip past him to balance the blanket on the basin and put his arms around her. And he could not fight it. She smiled at her daydreams, lolling against the shores of his sanity, and together they shuffled to the low armchair.

He lay awake and stared into his private sky. A giant coffee stain spread month by month across the plaster but his two eyes now disengaged themselves and he looked beyond onto a turbid plain. The chat show host quieted the audience respectfully and their applause conducted itself hurriedly through the overflow and into the cool day. The milk-white gulls wheeled endlessly on zephyr-wings, and the world was quiet.

Surely she was old, she also lived in his too-hampered world of aches and slow-loaded steps. He knew she looked ahead for hand rails and slept when she was bored. Yet the truth lived in his pockets now, and under the soles of his feet, and it told him she was more alive than he had ever been. The knowledge enthralled him and excited him. Instead of the regurgitated past, new ideas came into his eyes, and every old impression was overrun by younger thoughts.

New places, conversations, a new face, a beautiful face, smooth cheeks and dancing eyes that filled him with an ineffable happiness. He felt it then, held his breath, knew the fear that lurked in him was the fear of never meeting her again. He wanted to feel her arms around him, and lay his grey head against her collar bone and soak up her vehemence and never worry about the pounding rain again.

He made toast and filled the kettle somewhere just below his dreams and again their day rolled into dusk then dark without a sound. Irene's hands were cold and Bernard blew on them and rubbed them. He put his overcoat against the draft and willed the night to end.

Bernard put his hat on and went down into the day. He had to find a stove, and it was pension-day. The sky rammed his hat onto his ear-tops and spat at him. But he did not care. He ruthlessly dragged his reflection over shop-fronts and doorways, and denied the film-thin drizzle that tried to encrust his purpose. He was fiercely happy.

The Post Office sign was tiny under the over-size municipal building that housed it. Stunted saplings idled in wire casings in front of it.

And then, across the newly-fading pedestrian square, he saw her. A figure that descended the last step and disappeared across the road. His mind began to run but tripped over his age and the dormant arthritis that lay across his path, and he found himself in the same spot out of breath, and she had gone.

He could not follow, could not join her dance, and the choking stride of disappointment began to numb him. He collected the money, and left a notice on the classified board, and went to find her. Bernard knew now the keen futility of his desire. She was not part of his life. He could never share her, but he could only watch from the side, and that was good enough.

The never-ending mirror-world of shop-fronts ran behind him and he limped out of the town. He hoped to see her skirts sweeping ahead, drawing closer, whirring into each tiny droplet that refracted a thousand images of the emptiness ahead into his consciousness. He had no time to wipe away the mist, blundering on into the near-clouded distance.

Coming to the beach he cut across the dunes to approach the hut from behind. It was a haste-drawn hypotenuse that let him fall against an overhang and black sand fill his shoes. A last ridge and there was the raven-feathered roof crouched beneath the draught.

And stopped there in the wind, his hair tossing like a wave-crest and just as lost. Because there was a figure leaving, and a snide gust threw her cheerful words, "goodbye, see you tomorrow," like a blow across his body. He strained to see the man's face, tried to move round, his hands scraping at the slick sea-silt, and fell. The soft sand allowed him up again just once to see the blue-coated figure slip behind the grass waves, then crash against the breast-like mound.

That was Mr X, he knew. A son, a brother, a friend, social worker. Someone who knew her and she cared for and often talked with. She knew his face, his smile, his familiar greeting. He flailed, sending grains plummeting towards their accomplices in shaky wet handfuls, and fell and rose the whole way home. Indigo twilight slunk behind him through the streets. As he crossed their window, the fourteen eyes of the family that sat all night behind the take-away counter, followed him past and swivelled back as one to the television screen.

They had decided over breakfast long ago to live together for as long as possible, and so the flat rent inhaled most of their money without a second thought.

That morning Bernard stood beside Irene, telling her about the sea and for a while they drifted together in a lilting silence. They had saved many blithe summer moments and spent them on that giant adamantine playground, with each other and their children. Pier-end picnics and ship-spotting led to tiny dreams and nature-table offerings, and a solid equanimity had blown across them both.

He simply wanted to enjoy her company a while.
Hullo! Come in.
She had been leaning on the half-door when she saw him, and now held it open.
Thank you. He went in and sat down. She left the doors wide, letting the breeze tickle the threshold and refresh the dim interior.
Wonderful day isn't it? The weather really races across the sky.
Bernard cleared his throat.
I saw you in town the other day, but I couldn't catch you up.
Oh, I'm sorry. It is frustrating being old, isn't it? She chuckled like a child.
Do you actually live here?
Oh yes. I've been here over twelve years now. I have an arrangement with the council — I'm one less room in a home and they give me a small pension. My husband was a committee member.
And you're happy here? HE KNEW THE ANSWER.
I've got everything I need. The sea is much better than a television. No adverts! SHE LAUGHED AGAIN AND HE WAS TOUCHED.
A son? A brother?
Has Mr X been today? He looked out of the door to the ocean.
Oh yes, he comes every day, even Sundays sometimes.

HE IS HERE EVERY DAY.

Bernard pushed his spectacles up his nose and tried to see where the sea became clouds. A recondite point one arc of the world away swam in and out of his focus. His lenses were smooth-sided rock pools and the day dived and splashed across them.

Have you lived in this town all your life?

He nodded, his mind had gone out amongst the swell. It was falling down, rolling off the wave-rim towards the ever-deepening trough before it. And then it was caught and began a syncopated ascent, climbing back to her effortlessly and without thought.

Who is Mr X?

He's the postman. I get a lot of letters.

POSTMAN. He drew his eyes back into the room, and his irises flared in the dark.

Can I offer you some orange squash?

No thank you.

Shall we take a walk down to the pier, I need to go that way, if you'll forgive me.

Bernard gathered his power and smiled at her.

Shouldering her overcoat, she led the way down to the gravelled shore. He slipped slowly on the moist pebbles. His feet curled around each heavy-fleshed rock. And she picked her way beside him, tripping sometimes but never falling.

Isn't it the most wonderful noise?

Bernard looked aside to where the tissue-paper wave heads crashed and destroyed themselves on the coast. A screaming interface of two vastly different worlds, the water soaked up by the dunes and the stones thrown about by the sea. Sea-weeds flapped about the pier supports and the surf splashed its belly. There were slime-covered steps leading onto its black-bruised back. His shoes seemed part of the wood he balanced on. He was tired, and insubstantial against the great structure he clung to. High limpets huddled deeper inside their shells as he passed, urging the tempest away.

I'm just going in here, I won't be long.

She turned to go into the pier house.

I have to go back, I'm sorry.

She faced him, hair whipped across an astral map that shone defiant.

Well, see you soon then.

They stood until a squall-hurled gull scythed between them, slicing the tableau apart.

There was a blockage in the shower, but Bernard could not bend far enough to grasp the metallic surround. His glasses threw themselves from the bridge of his nose and clattered into the scum-skinned water.

He pushed the sodden towel around the slick with his foot once more, and went and lay down. In the other room he heard Irene give a mouse-sneeze and the rush of a blanket cascading to the floor. She would not notice, wouldn't complain. The ceiling-stain was dim, and the daylight slid mistrustfully through the window. He suddenly realised that this was a colourless space, and pulled himself off the bed to replace his shoes. On his way out he folded the rug back over the sleeper and straightened his hat-brim to perfection.

The newsagents were full of red-gold cards, tawdry insults to sincerity and season. They spread down the wall in rows, like brightly coloured vomit. He searched behind them for more modest pictures. There were some fine dogs, and geese amongst cream leaves. One was a colourful pencil drawing of a castle in the sun and he choose that.

Irene liked it a lot. He knew because she turned it in her hands and pressed it between her smudge-thumbs. He left her sleeping with the cardboard castle tucked against her chin. He went and sat on the toilet, arching his back into the cold cistern, trying to straighten, strengthen himself. The foul water in the corner was disappearing imperceptibly. When he looked down, it had gone.

The next morning he went back to the post office to see if she was there, and if anyone had replied to his notice. He sat waiting by the stamp machine for an hour, enjoying the sitting. Then he asked about the stove. Two people had left numbers, and he rang from the open booth by Parcels. The first was unobtainable and the second said she could drop it round next Thursday, for £12. Heavy coins fell unresounding into the machine as he replaced the handset. She was not here.

A rocking chair. The rocking chair. Why was it here? On the pavement?
Digging his feet into the duckboards, he skidded between the dunes. And there she was, coming up towards him.
Hullo there! I must catch the last post, do you mind if we go back up?
She waved an envelope in her left hand.
Why is your chair on the road?
Oh, Mr X put it up there for me.
Why?
I'm tidying up.
They had reached the road, and set off obliquely in the direction of a faint dark dot they both knew was the box. He had sent postcards to his parents from this box that stood alone, a mass of red-cast metal impervious to time and change.
There. She patted the old thing. It'll be dark soon, you should get home you know, these days…
HE COULDN'T STAY.

I don't mind. His mind pleaded through his eyes, wishing her into submission.

I don't think its a very good idea.

NO. NO.

Then I'll see you soon.

Yes. Goodbye.

She span away and cut immediately into the rippling sward. He stood watching her bob in and out of the dunes, ever fainter in the dying light. For a time the lee of the box was a safe place, then a gust reached around it and drove him homewards.

The next week a storm raged. It threw all its taurine force against the town, lashing rain and cloud into the river-roads and alleyways. Giant plastic decorations swung and plummeted onto granite kerbs and globules of mascara inched down women's faces.

Bernard lost his hat on the way to post Christmas cards, watching it cruise away into the crazed day. Snatched blasts of icy air blew in and out of the overflow. Irene slept in a meadow beside a castle. The weather got worse. Incessant rain belched out by the boiling clouds leapt towards the earth, bins and deckchairs clawing at passage walls for a reprieve before they were thrown off again. He saw a starling, come loose from its perch, dashed against the window, one black eye pressed horribly into the glass before it fell caesura-necked out of sight.

He had a card for Anne, but it was impossible to leave the flat. He lay and listened to the 'open' sign slapping the glass door below the window and into his mind came the streets that wound towards the sea. He walked through them on sun-days, when the sky was azure and the coast shone gently back at the light, arm in arm with a new plan. A firm calm that pervaded his frame soothed his senses and he fell asleep.

The morning of the sixth day came without rain. Sun shone quickly and was then smacked back behind the thick wisps that sped across the sky on their way to war. But as he rose to go, coal-filled clouds tumbled from above and suffocated the light. He waited all day for a respite, but none came. Finally he cracked and, tucking Irene into bed, went out into half-day.

A steady gale ignored the seething ocean and glanced off the shore. Bernard stood by the post box, looking out to where the waves skewed into the pier and exploded. There was soft-flowing sand hardening in the gutter and he saw one of the duckboards on the far side of the road. He began to fear.

The tight sand was so wet it was easy to walk on and soon he felt the old stones beating against his soles. Ahead he saw planks, and a sheet, and he ran. The hut had gone. Its concrete base was strewn with wood, and looking up to the dunes Bernard saw more debris. The sun-blenched curtain still on its rail was wound round one of the boxes, and he saw the side had been smashed in. There was nothing else he could see. He clambered onto the block and pulled away at the splinter-drenched board. His hands pushed into something heavy and sodden. Bringing it into the gloom he saw that it was paper. A mass of fibre, reclaimed by the water, dropping onto his feet. He threw it aside, reaching deeper and found dry sheets. They were envelopes, her letters. Who were they from? Who wrote so often, who knew her so well?

His fingers were clumsy with cold, too thick and too veined to touch the pale flesh. But at last he had one, unfolded in the gathering dusk. It was addressed to Anne, he moved his glasses with his knuckles, reading again. A journey, nice weather, missing you, the wind flipped it over, signed "Charles", written three years before. He opened another, the same, written the next day. A birthday card, letters and more letters. He strained to see the shapes that crawled across the ash-papers, and knew where he had seen that spider's scrawl before. The disintegrating leaves sagged at their final betrayal, and abandoned Bernard to stand confused under the ebon sky that battled round him. He felt utter loss, and waste and emptiness, bellowing at the air with untutored rage.

The wind fell hungrily on the carrion that lay limp over his fingers, and the earth lost interest and turned away from the sun. Then the darkness came across the sea, swallowing paper and words with its ink, and destroyed her for the last time.

Catherine Totty

contributors

Contributors

Stephanie Frank is at Mansfield College, Oxford.

Tamar Landau is a graduate student at Corpus Christi College, Oxford. By day she is an ancient historian. By night she dances tango. Her first book was published in her native Israel in 1994.

Alex Lawrence is a Classicist at Christ Church, Oxford. His tastes are eclectic, his actions dynamic, his ego frantic, his family ecstatic, his finances burassic. Now hurry up and read the story.

Frank Shovlin is from Donegal Town, Ireland and is writing up a D. Phil. in English at St John's College, Oxford. His story ***Dead Boy*** appeared in the 1998 Short Stories May Anthology.

Simon Stirrup was born and raised in south-east London, where he went to school and still lives with his family. He is currently studying Natural Sciences at Fitzwilliam College, Cambridge.

Catherine Totty is in her first year reading Physics at Brasenose College, Oxford. Her private passions include writing, breeding gerbils and crusader castles. The rest of her time is consumed by directing plays.

Rachel Tripp is in her second year at Girton College, Cambridge.

Meg Vandermerwe is at St. Hilda's College, Oxford.

Richard Williams, 21, is a final year student at Downing College, Cambridge. This is his first story to be published since his return from his 15 year sabbatical. Thanks McCabe, Julie, Graham.